Praise

"Timeless wisdom on many levels, wrapped within an absolutely beautifully-told story! The insights you'll gain through this wonderful read will be exceeded only by the total joy you will experience while reading it. If I may suggest, purchase a copy for everyone you love. They will benefit greatly, as well as thank you profusely."

—***Bob Burg***,
co-author of the international bestseller,
The Go-Giver

The Way of the Three-Year-Old Why

Live What Really Matters

Donn King

Hidden Mentor Media

Copyright © 2023 by Donn King

All rights reserved.

No part of this publication may be reproduced, distributed, or transmitted in any form or by any means, including photocopying, recording, or other electronic or mechanical methods, without the prior written permission of the publisher, except as permitted by U.S. copyright law. For permission requests, contact donn@donnking.com.

The story and characters in this business fable are fictitious. Certain real-life locations are recognizable. The story is based on the real-life circumstances of the author and his family. It is not, however, autobiographical. Many of the specific details are completely fictitious. Do not assume anything you read here is factual.

Book Cover by 100 Covers

Illustrations by Donn King

First edition 2023

ISBN 979-8-9893121-0-8 (ebook)
ISBN 979-8-9893121-1-5 (paperback)
ISBN 979-8-9893121-2-2 (hardcover)

Published by
Hidden Mentor Media
257 N. Calderwood St. #327
Alcoa, TN 37701

DonnKing.com

Contents

Dedication	VII
Foreword	IX
1. The Beginning of the Beginning	1
2. The First Three-Year-Old Guideline	14
3. The Second Three-Year-Old Guideline	30
4. The Third Three-Year-Old Guideline	43
5. The Fourth Three-Year-Old Guideline	52
6. The Fifth Three-Year-Old Guideline	68
7. The Beginning of the Ending	82
8. The Five Guidelines	101
Author's Notes	103
Discussion Guide	107
First chapter of Real Speak	111
Acknowledgements	121
About the Author	125
Special coffee offer	127

For Hannah, who cannot talk but cannot help but inspire.
And for Janet, who lights up every day.

Foreword

Remember, for a second, sitting in a classroom from your high school or college days. Recall the people in the room with you. Can you still picture the surroundings? Are the sounds and smells making their way back into the cinema of your mind?

Were you excited?

Were you bored?

Were you sleepy?

Allow your imagination to go further. The teacher has just walked into the room and the lecture is about to begin. What was the name of the instructor? Did you love them? Was the class that came to mind your favorite subject? Or was it not really your top choice–but your friends in the same room made the whole thing memorable?

If the field of study that popped up for you wasn't so great–was it a course in which you struggled? Did you dislike the material or the teacher?

Now, as you remember that setting, ask yourself; what brought that specific classroom into the forefront for you?

For most, the answer is rooted in emotions.

If the emotions you experienced at the time were negative, the subject itself is most likely not your favorite. However, if the emotions were positive in nature, even if it was an extremely hard course, you tend to look back on that particular class as being one of your most beloved.

Whether you loved it or hated it, you can likely trace your lifelong relationship with that academic area to the classroom experience itself–and the emotions you felt at the time–rather than whether you mastered or struggled with the material.

Think about your favorite subject. Did your love for the course happen because of a teacher who brought it to life? Maybe they turned boring facts into thrilling adventures. Or did a family member who loved the same area of study inspire you–and their zeal made you an enthusiast by bloodline?

When considering why we loved certain classes, our answers usually have very little to do with the academic subject. Instead, the reasons are almost always about the person who engaged our mind. Their creativity, their passion, and their stories turned lessons into epic adventures. We relished the experience. And as we think back about them now, their voice may still be there–whispering wisdom into our memories.

When my teachers were great spinners of classroom tales, I listened, I learned, and I loved the lessons. Their impact was so powerful, and their methods so endearing, I actually lost track of the fact I was learning things; it just happened.

I love superb storytellers–and Donn King is one of the very best. For me, he's a bit of Mark Twain, with a pinch of Lewis Grizzard, mixed in with a heaping helping of my favorite teachers.

You are about to embark on a journey that I believe you will thoroughly enjoy. The characters are lovable, the storyline will grab you–keeping you engaged until the very end, and you'll learn principles which have the power to improve your life. This story will stay with you long after the last page has turned.

Donn's voice will resonate with you.

His years as an associate professor of communication, his tenure as a pastor, and his unique perspective from a life filled with both triumph and struggle have prepared his heart to craft a narrative that will touch your soul.

Donn has unquestionably secured his place at the parable author's table, and I must say, I'm genuinely honored to share the same space with him and call him my friend.

So, dear reader, I am excited for you! The encounter you are about to have is going to be amazing. Relax, read, and completely immerse yourself in *The Way of the Three-Year-Old Why*. I trust the experience will be as meaningful to you as it has been for me.

I'll see you on the other side–my heart already all aflutter, just like yours will be.

~Jeff C. West, Bestselling and award-winning author of *The Unexpected Tour Guide*, and coauthor of the multi-award-winning sales parable, *Said the Lady with the Blue Hair*

Chapter One

The Beginning of the Beginning

Monday, May 15

"I'm glad I could find another speaker for you," Dan Roberts said into his headset, while the other coffee shop patrons politely ignored him. "I was really looking forward to working with your group, and I appreciate your understanding. Keep me in mind for next year?"

"We would love to have you," said Gavin Harrison. "You obviously have some great material, and you could help our middle managers ramp up their speaking skills. I gotta tell you, though.... I completely understand why you have to back out, but this is the second time. I'm going to have trouble selling the idea of booking you again."

Dan swallowed hard, but he kept the weariness out of his voice and said, "I know. And I appreciate your going to bat for me. I think we could make a big difference to your membership, but I know it's hard to deal with the uncertainty. Maybe we should explore some other way of working together?"

"Definitely. Who knows, we might come up with something we can do over Zoom sometime. By the way, a word to the wise among friends? Your website is getting dated. It would help me advocate for you if you can get some more recent material up there."

"You're right," Dan said, "and I appreciate the reminder. I've had that on my 'to do list' for months. It's just that with all the medical stuff...."

"Oh, I understand! I hope things go well at the hospital!"

Dan had carefully kept a slight smile on his face during the conversation, even though it was audio only. He knew body language influences not just the audience but the speaker. After all, helping people communicate effectively was his expertise. But when the call ended, he let out a heavy sigh and slumped in his chair.

At that moment, Dan looked older than his 65 years. A little over six feet tall, in recent years, gravity had colluded with arthritis in his hips. Even five years ago, people had had trouble keeping up with him as he walked, but he seemed to have aged 20 years in the last 10. Still, he came back to life when he spoke on stage, moving and gesturing fluidly, and the years dropped away.

But he wasn't on stage now.

You DON'T understand, he thought.

"Rough morning?" someone behind him said.

Dan turned to see a new barista wheeling a cart toward the coffee counter. She looked a little over five feet tall, but with sinewy arms and capable hands. Long, curly, bronze-colored hair cascaded to her shoulders. Light pink lipstick complemented her complexion. Her eyebrows formed neat arches, drawing attention to her almond-shaped eyes and high cheekbones. She projected a sense of peacefulness and gracefulness. He had not seen her before, although he came into The Blissful Bean Coffee Haven two or three times a week to make uninterrupted phone calls and work on speeches while enjoying his favorite brew.

He smiled sadly. "I'm afraid so. I got this gig six months ago, but I've had to bail out at the last minute since my daughter is having surgery."

Dan was used to people reacting to such news with pity, which he didn't want, or with advice, which he also didn't want. He tried to deflect such questions to avoid an extended conversation, but something about this barista led him to open up a bit.

"I'm so sorry to hear that!" she said. "Juggling that sort of thing makes it hard to take care of business."

Dan nodded. "It's not the first time it's happened, either. Just gotta deal."

"I don't mean to pry, but... you're Dan, right?"

He smiled. The staff at The Blissful Bean were always friendly and professional, but with a couple of exceptions, most didn't connect with customers beyond recognizing the regulars and their favorite drinks and food. The job had too much turnover, college kids on their way through. Dan taught clients to connect with people on a personal level as much as possible as a way of standing out from the crowd. Now here was someone practicing just that.

"That's right. How did you know?"

"Sean, my manager, told me about some of our regulars, and he mentioned you were a speaker of some sort who worked here a lot. My name is Callie, by the way."

"Nice to meet you, Callie. And, yes, I speak—but not as much as I'd like to. I'm afraid my daughter's issues are chronic, and it makes it hard to be dependable."

Dan braced for the next question, the usual one of "what do you speak about?" or "what kind of issues does your daughter have?" He had his positioning statement ready to go, anticipating the typical "I could never stand up in front of a crowd and talk" and "how do you get your ideas?" and "is there much money in that?" or his stock answers concerning Hope's genetic disorder.

But Callie just nodded and kept listening. Her eyes were deep pools of nearly all black, not staring, not flirtatious, but unhurried, as if she had all the time in the world. She smiled slightly. After a comfortable minute of silence, Dan continued speaking.

"I hate not being dependable. I'm fortunate that I've had a supportive day job for years teaching college students. When Hope winds up in the hospital, I can hold classes online or have them work on out-of-class assignments. I love my job, but what I've wanted to do for 30 years is to speak professionally full time. I help other people communicate effectively, and speaking makes me feel alive. And why am I telling you this, anyway?" He smiled. "I can't imagine that it matters to you."

She smiled back. "I have that effect on people, it seems. It actually runs in the family. And I'm fascinated with what makes people come alive. It's one reason I love working in a coffee shop. I get to meet all kinds of people that I otherwise wouldn't. Thank you for sharing that with me!"

She gave a friendly nod, said, "I'll bet you'll work through the difficulties! I have a good feeling about it." She turned back to her cart, and wheeled it toward the kitchen behind the coffee counter.

That was interesting, Dan thought. He hadn't felt as listened to in the last six months as he had just then. *How did she do that?* He wondered out of professional interest since he helped others achieve that. But he also enjoyed the warmth of simply being understood—not pitied, not patronized, and not interrogated.

***

Tuesday, May 16

Dan looked at his WordPress template for the tenth time and thought, *I need to just pick a new one.* He remembered the conversation he had with Ana just last week.

"I know nothing about the tech under it," she'd said. "But I know you've had that website for 20 years. I hate to say it, but it looks it, too. Do you think that might impede new business?"

Ironic, since Ana was the least techy person he knew. She had finally reluctantly consented to get a cell phone only six months prior, and she still had trouble figuring out the difference between it and a cordless phone. ("Don't I have to be close to a base unit to use it?")

But if even *she* thought his website needed sprucing up, it needed sprucing up.

He opened up the laptop on the dining room table he used as an office when he worked at home, the house phone close at hand in case either Grace or one of Hope's nurses needed something. Interruptions drove him crazy, but his sense of responsibility led him to make sure the people who needed him could reach him. He hoped updating the website wouldn't take his full attention.

He poked around in the free templates, trying to find one that would look better than the one he'd been using. It had been state-of-the-art when he first installed it, but he had kept it through multiple WordPress upgrades, electing to keep prior editor versions, cobbling together menus. Now his site looked dated on a computer and horrible on a cell phone.

The first template he picked looked decent except... *Oh, God! Every single old blog post is showing up on the sidebar!* Posts about Second Life and higher education and every kind of mishmash that had struck his interest over the years lined up, leaving the impression of complete scatter. *I have to fix this immediately!* But how?

Just then, the intercom buzzed.

Dan groaned.

He loved his wife, Grace, dearly, but she had a knack of calling at just exactly the wrong time.

Impatiently, he picked up the handset and gruffly said, "Yes?"

THE WAY OF THE THREE-YEAR-OLD WHY

"Honey, I'm sorry, I hate to disturb you," she said. "But I dropped my glasses and I can't reach them. Can you please come get them for me?"

Pause, then, "I'll be right there." The website would have to wait. Probably no one would see it in the meantime anyway, since his traffic had dropped over the last five years. Still, he hated for anyone to see it all scattered and exposed.

But Grace couldn't retrieve the glasses herself, and without them she couldn't function.

Dan remembered when Grace had been the most the active of the two of them. If she wanted the living room rearranged, he would come home and find it done—no "honey do" jokes for him. In fact, Grace ran rings around Dan, always moving, getting five goals accomplished in the time it took him to start on one. That made it even harder when arthritis robbed her of much movement and then put her in the wheelchair.

He spent more time at the coffee shop these days because he hated the interruptions. But he couldn't resent them. He sighed, jotted a quick note to remember where he was in the complex updating operation, and went to retrieve her glasses in the bedroom where she now spent her days.

"Did you see the latest on the coronation in England?" Grace asked as soon as he entered. "They just released the official portraits, and there's one with William, but none with Harry."

She talked more about the royal festivities continuing after the May 6 ceremony, Dan smiling and half listening while he turned over the website challenges in his mind. Grace seldom complained, but she needed his company to ease her isolation. Whenever he could take time away from his business, teaching class, or caring for Hope, Grace talked about anything and everything. Honestly, he loved the time he spent with her, listening to her enthusiasms, watching her draw or paint, or watching old black and white movies. It tempted him to quit everything and just spend his days with her.

After all, they had planned carefully for retirement. Between his retirement fund and Social Security for them both, they could live comfortably. Why not just throw in the towel?

But whenever Dan suggested such, Grace shook her head vehemently. "No! If you did that, you would wish you had kept at it. You would look at me and think, 'She did this to me.' You would wind up resenting me and all my problems. You have enough to deal with making sure Hope gets cared for. You need to keep working."

"You're not here, are you?" she said.

Dan focused, realized she had asked something he hadn't heard. "I'm sorry, hon. It's just that I'm trying to fix an issue with the website, and I'm distracted. I should have been listening. What did you say?"

"Never mind," she said. "It wasn't important anyway. Go back to what you were doing."

Sheepishly, Dan left the bedroom. He sat back down in the dining room chair, said out loud to no one in particular, "Let's see, where was I?"

THE WAY OF THE THREE-YEAR-OLD WHY

The intercom buzzed, this time from Hope's room. He took a moment to remember which nurse cared for Hope today, then answered.

"Whatcha need, Liana?"

"Mr. Roberts? I'm sorry to bother you, but we are out of one of her seizure meds."

"Is it due now?" he asked, knowing it was 2 PM and definitely time for it.

"Yes sir, I'm afraid so."

He sighed. "OK, just a minute." Up from the chair once again, his hips complaining, he went to the refrigerator, snagged the fresh bottle, and took it to Hope's room.

A small bedroom, they had retrofitted it with a counter and sink, multiple storage cabinets, equipment shelving, and its own electrical system to avoid overwhelming the main house current. Anytime someone new came into the little enclave, they always remarked on "a little hospital room." They had converted the guest bedroom next door into a medical storage facility, packed with supplies like urinary catheters, enteral feed bags, cables, suction catheters, cases of liquid nourishment, circuits for breathing machines, and tons of girly clothes that would fit a typical six-year-old.

Dan paused in the doorway and waited for Liana to finish suctioning Hope's trach. Some of those small clothes lay on the Leckey PAL seat, ready to put on his 20-year-old daughter. Liana cleared the suction catheter and smiled at Dan. "Thank you!"

He handed her the cold brown bottle, but he kept looking at Hope. "You know, she ought to be going out with friends now, living in a dorm instead of this room."

Liana's smile turned sad, and she said, "I know. But it's a minor miracle she is still with you."

"Yes, you're right. I can't help but wonder, though. What does she dream about? I dream about flying. Does she dream about walking? Does she dream at all?"

Choking up, he turned without another word and headed back to the laptop. He shook his head, pushing his feelings down. *WordPress waits for no man,* he thought. *Maybe there's another theme that will just hide that sidebar altogether.*

He found a minimalist theme in the list, clicked to make it active. It worked! But now the photo that had appeared at the top had vanished, leaving an odd blank space behind.

The doorbell rang. A delivery of oxygen equipment.

Dan sighed, closed the laptop, and answered the front door.

***

Grace heard the doorbell, and she could almost feel Dan's sigh. She knew interruptions constantly punctuated his day, and she ached to do something about it—to do *anything*, really. Dan would be happy to sit and listen to a stream with a hot cup of coffee, but Grace always wanted to be painting, making stained glass, building furniture.

Until the arthritis had robbed her of all that.

She looked around the small bedroom at her paintings festooning the walls, the bookshelves she had crafted, the handwoven wall hangings. Grace understood Dan's creative urges and shared in them, but they each expressed them differently. Though she enjoyed making graphics on the computer, it just didn't quite satisfy the tactile needs she had for hands-on work.

She heard Dan out on the porch talking to the delivery guy. He tried, Lord knows he tried, but she ached to help with Hope's caretaking duties, especially since Dan couldn't keep track of all the disparate needs for them all.

Her eyes landed on the twin wood carvings on the shelf by the door, and she smiled at the memory of the workshop weekend she had gifted Dan for an anniversary. He always wanted to carve the traditional Appalachian spirit faces that filled artisan shops outside Gatlinburg, and it seemed a fun activity they could do together back before the arthritis took over.

Carving had come naturally to Grace, but Dan struggled to make his hands do what his brain wanted them to do. Her carving, a first-time effort, looked as accomplished as anything in those artisan shops, but Dan's had looked hacked out with an axe by a five-year-old. He even tried a second time with a fresh piece of wood, but his second effort looked even more childish—demented, even. They had laughed together, and Dan insisted on displaying the two next to each other. But he had given his set of carving tools to his nephew and never mentioned wanting to carve again.

A couple of years later, arthritis claimed her hands, her back, and her hips with a vengeance, and she could no longer wield carving tools or paint brushes with any precision and without pain. An assistive technology trackball allowed her to work on a computer with some dexterity, and speech recognition software reduced the need for keyboarding. But no computer could hold tools on her behalf, and so she left painting, carving, and crocheting behind.

The door opened and Dan came in holding the supply delivery ticket.

"I think we got everything," he said, "but honestly, I can't make heads or tails of this paperwork. Can you check it over?"

"Sure. Ummm, can you hand me my glasses, the ones you were going to get for me on the last trip? They fell on the floor."

"Oops! I'm sorry, I should have gotten them last time." He picked up the glasses and handed them to her, along with the stack of papers.

She took the pink NCR forms, ran through them quickly, and then said, "I don't see anything on here about suction catheters. Did they not include them?"

Dan groaned and smacked his forehead. "I didn't even think to ask about them. I'm sorry. Can you call them? I'm going to run to The Blissful Bean for a few minutes so I can focus on the website redesign."

Grace hated making phone calls. She thought Dan handled those better. But she knew he had been trying to focus on business, and that he worried about their finances moving into retirement.

So she said, "I guess. I'll check to see what's going on. Probably an insurance thing."

"Thanks, hon!" he gave her a quick kiss and headed out the door, leaving her to wish for the way things had once been when she could beat him to the car. She picked up the phone and painfully punched in the numbers for the medical equipment supplier and then waited patiently as the tired, familiar hold music cycled through and a mechanical voice assured her of the importance of her call.

Chapter Two

The First Three-Year-Old Guideline

Wednesday morning, May 17

Dan sipped his coffee—good, even though it had gone cold. He usually began his coffeehouse working sessions by flipping through email and responding to anything "on fire" so he could concentrate on creating material. Today, that didn't seem so important. He had already prepped the material for the communication workshop he had lined up a week from Friday. His next keynote was scheduled in two months—too far off to know what the nursing schedule would look like, close enough to make it hard to find a replacement speaker.

He considered the best use of his work time as he looked around the familiar space of The Blissful Bean. From his favorite table near an electrical outlet, he could see over half the shop and knew it as well as his own home.

The Blissful Bean actually comprised three levels of an old warehouse. The retail coffee house lived at ground level on the middle floor, with the roastery in the basement and the office/meeting room level upstairs.

Ancient hardwood scarred by unknown machinery formed the coffeehouse floor. Eclectic tables of different sizes filled the space, some intimate, some large. Booths with padded seats lined the front windows, while the back had two "conversation pits" with overstuffed leather chairs and sofas in front of a fireplace. Close to the front sat a small raised stage with a piano. At one time the coffeehouse had featured live music and open-mike night, but now the stage held a couple more tables and a sign saying, "Please don't play the piano." Close by, the owner's original red roaster, with which he began experimenting with batches of coffee beans, presided in retirement.

Dan recognized the regulars amidst the soft overhead lighting. Pictures of coffee cherries, coffee beans, coffee flowers, and coffee farmers adorned most walls, interspersed with exhibitions of local artists.

Maybe this would be a good time to get the website finally working properly, Dan thought. In years past, Dan had designed entire web sites in PHP, but he quickly became bored with the routine of debugging code. He couldn't yet justify paying someone else to take care of his website, but he tried to make do with easily available templates.

Hope's nursing schedule had recently had hardly any gaps, just an occasional night shift every couple of weeks. But one nurse had been talking about possibly moving into a clinical setting for higher pay. More than once, Dan had to cancel a speaking gig or workshop at the last minute because a nurse quit.

That worried him. His upcoming keynote fell just about at the time Hope's next bronchoscopy came due, and he had little to no leeway on scheduling that.

He thought about simply canceling everything, giving up on marketing, letting the website go altogether. Still, with retirement looming and his responsibility to "keep the income incoming," he needed to pick up more speeches and workshops. *I should at least have a basic working website*, he thought.

Eventually basic program and content information loaded correctly, and he returned to email despite the site's less-than-perfect appearance

One hundred fifty-two emails, he thought, *and just about every one of them wanting me to buy something*. He highlighted and selected them all, going through the list then unselecting the rare email that deserved more attention. With one click, he could delete the ones he didn't really need to read.

Then he saw it, just before hitting the delete button—the email from a client he had pursued for three years! It came from Elizabeth Martinez, the VP of Sales for Agile Manufacturing, the one person at the company with the real ability to hire a speaker. She asked about his availability to speak at a company gathering *and* to conduct an in-depth follow-up workshop for company executives.

Yes! he thought.

But then he paused, wrinkled his brow, and opened his calendar in another tab. He groaned. The date of the meeting fell the week after the upcoming keynote. He needed the gig, had pursued it for three years, but now he hesitated. The looming bronchoscopy concerned him.

He doodled for a few minutes, then exited through the coffee shop's back door. He took out his cell phone and dialed Ana.

"Can I pick your brain a minute?" he said when she answered.

"Yeah, if you don't mind me cooking while we talk." He heard pans rattling in the background.

"Sure, no problem! I just need your advice. This company I've really wanted to work with contacted me for a keynote and workshop, but it's in a couple of months. Pre-pandemic, they would have been working at least six months to a year ahead, and I wouldn't have even considered it, what with Hope's issues. But now it's almost doable. Almost. I'm not sure. What would you do?"

"What I would do is not have kids," she said. "But that ship has not only already sailed, it's already crossed the ocean and unloaded its cargo. How much are we talking about?"

Dan named the fee. Ana whistled. "Dang, man, you could really use that. Why haven't you already bagged it?"

He paused, asking himself the same question. God knew he could use the money.

"What happens if I'm away, and a nurse calls out? Hope can't stay by herself, and Grace can't take care of her. What if I'm a six-hour plane flight away? Plus, it's the week after another gig I've accepted, so that makes it even more likely some nursing calendar issue will come up. If Murphy's Law pops up, they're screwed. I'm screwed! I've been doing these things over Zoom the last three years, though nothing of this magnitude. This one will require serious travel and time away."

Long pause. He heard a kitchen timer go off, followed by the sound of running water. Then she said, "Hmmmm. Do you already have a connection with the meeting planner?"

"We've talked casually over the last couple of years, but nothing significant. I've done the usual reaching out every month or two, sharing articles of interest and sending links to updated videos. She obviously sees something interesting, but we've never met in person."

"Does she know about Hope?"

"I think so.... I'm uncertain, actually. I've talked about Hope and her challenges in some videos the planner has seen."

"What would happen if you wrote her an email explaining your interest and also your hesitation? Maybe have a Plan B in place, like a Zoom workshop."

Dan had walked down to the little creek running behind The Blissful Bean. A couple of ducks floated leisurely against the current, occasionally dipping underneath the water to consume a morsel. The scene and the sound helped Dan clear his mind as he considered Ana's advice.

"That might work! Giving up the keynote means losing most of the fee. But it's safer and still profitable, and it would save them travel expenses."

"Just be prepared for her to dump the whole thing. I don't know. It's my idea, I know, but I'm not sure I'd want to take that chance."

"Thanks, Ana. You've given me something to think about, like always."

"Any time. Now I need to get back to ruining supper."

***

Dan suddenly realized how long he had been away from his table. He had never had to worry about anything getting lost or stolen at The Blissful Bean. Everyone seemed to look out for each other, and at least twice someone had turned in something he left behind—a pair of headphones, even an iPad. But all his essential livelihood tools sat unattended, and for more than enough time for someone to gather them up and be long gone.

He hurried back in and saw with relief everything sitting right where he had left it, with Callie approaching with a fresh cup of coffee in one hand, a carafe in the other, and a smile.

"I saw you out back on the phone, and figured you'd like a refill when you returned," she said. "Looked pretty intense there for a while."

"Thank you! Yes, this is perfect timing. Thanks for keeping an eye on things."

"My pleasure! You might say it's in my job description, keeping an eye on things. Coffee helps the creative process. Here you go!"

"Again, thanks! I need a clear head these days."

Dan told Callie about his recent opportunity and his hesitation, wondering why he felt so trusting of this relative stranger, but dismissing it as he responded to her thoughtful questions.

"How does Grace feel about this?" Callie asked.

"She's OK with it, says we don't have to have the money, but she may just be humoring me. She really wants me to be happy, and I appreciate that, but sometimes I think she hides her own wants. Bringing home the money is about the only thing I can do to try to make *her* happy, since I can't get rid of her arthritis, and I can't give her back her artistic activities. At least I can buy things to make her happy. That's why I feel like I just need to keep making as much money as I can."

"What does that cost *you*, though?"

Dan sighed. "I have to admit, I feel like I'm burning out. I can't tell you how long it's been since I did something just for the fun of it."

"Looks like you need a warmup. Here, set your cup over here."

Callie set the small airpot on the table, and Dan put his cup under the spout. Callie pushed down the lever on top, but no coffee came out, only the sputtering air from an empty carafe.

"Maybe you've heard before that you can't pour from an empty pitcher. Or an empty airpot." She smiled again.

"Yeah, some people have reminded of that." He chuckled. "Sometimes it seems like I've forgotten how to do anything but pour, though."

"Does Grace get her cup filled by your efforts?"

Dan looked out the front window and considered. Outside at the sidewalk tables, a couple sat holding hands and chatting. At another table, a college student sat with a large sketchpad, coffee beside her, drawing the outlines of a scene featuring the old bridge visible through the window.

"Not really," he said. "She appreciates it, enjoys whatever I bring home for a little while, but it winds up just taking up space. It's like nothing is ever enough."

Callie followed his gaze out the front window and said, "Grace is an artist, isn't she? What would happen if you brought her some art material?"

Dan tried to remember telling Callie about Grace's artistic bent, or, for that matter, telling Callie Grace's name. But he had probably rambled that information without thinking about it, and anyway, it was accurate. "I think it would just frustrate her, to tell you the truth. I mean, she already has plenty of that sort of thing. She just can't use it anymore—can't hold the brushes and such, can't sit in front of a canvas for long, that sort of thing."

"She uses a computer, though, right? You know they have graphics tablets now that can do incredible things in a small space, and they make adaptive grips to help people with challenges handle the pens. That might be something she wouldn't tire of, and it would feed her soul the way art always has for her."

Dan looked thoughtful. "You know, that sounds like a super idea! I haven't surprised her for a while now, and that could be a real game changer. Thanks, Callie! I'll do a little research and order one right now. I'll bet I could get one by the weekend."

"Glad to help! And good luck on deciding how to handle that whole speaking opportunity thing! I will leave you to it."

Callie took his empty cup and headed to the kitchen with it, leaving Dan to learn about graphics tablets and adaptive pen holders.

***

The house was quiet, a little too quiet for Grace. She kept the TV talking to itself for company and background noise, but it didn't satisfy like working in the little wood shop out back or helping Dan in the kitchen. Liana and Hope may have been just down the hall, but Hope couldn't talk at all, and Liana had her hands full in caring for Hope. With Dan gone to The Blissful Bean Coffee Haven, she might as well have been home by herself.

A baseball game filled the silence while leaving her free to wrestle with the household spreadsheet.

Grace always wanted Dan to do the bills along with her, mainly for the companionship, but he had little patience for or knowledge of the household finances. Besides (he said), handling the money was something she could do, whereas she could no longer mow the yard as she desired or help take care of Hope. So (he said), it made sense for her to do that and other work she *could* do while he took care of what she *couldn't*.

She had to admit it made sense. That didn't make it any more satisfying. Grace gladly contributed to the wellbeing of the household, but she hated dealing with all those numbers, and she so much missed her old activities.

Her phone rang. She saw it was Dan. *Probably forgot something*, she thought. *That man would forget to dress if I didn't remind him.* She muted the TV and answered.

"Hi, sweetie," he said. "I just bounced an idea off Ana, and I wonder what you might think about it. I have a chance at a pretty big fee, but I'm not sure I should take it, and I was thinking about offering something more dependable for a lower fee. Do you think we could afford it if I did that?"

You could quit right now, and we would be OK. But I don't want to discourage you.

"Why don't you want to take it? I mean, sure, we can afford it, but…. Is this something you really want to do?"

"Tell you the truth, I'm not sure. It's something I've been working toward for a long time, but I'm worried about the timing. What if Hope's bronchoscopy falls during the time of the event? I could wind up having to cancel last minute, just like I did for the speech I was supposed to do Friday."

"Can they move the event?"

"They won't move the event just to accommodate me. I'm sure they already have hotels and meeting rooms booked, people with airplane tickets bought. No, scaling back the offer would give them something useful while keeping my options open. Would you really be OK if I turned down the big ticket?"

"Whatever makes you happy, hon. We don't need the money."

"You're the best! I'll make a counterproposal, then. I'd just feel better about it. They could replace me easier for that than if I can't make the keynote. Plus, if they schedule me for a virtual session, I can probably do that from the hospital if need be. I love you!"

"I love you too!" she said. *And I miss you. I miss us.*

Dan hung up. Silence descended again. With a sigh, Grace unmuted the TV, now extolling the virtues of some exercise device, and turned back to the spreadsheet.

***

Wednesday afternoon, May 17

Dan absently worked his fork around in the salmon keto bowl while he continued trying to focus on his screen. The email seemed clunky, and he sought a more succinct way to propose the virtual workshop to Elizabeth Martinez. He wasn't even sure yet he would send it. His fork came up with nothing but lettuce—he had eaten all the good stuff without noticing.

Time for a pastry boost, he thought. Along with outstanding coffee and tea, The Blissful Bean offered light breakfast and lunch fare along with an array of muffins, cookies, macaroons, and parfaits. Midafternoon on a day of marketing emails and social media posts often offered a perfect time for a slice of lemon loaf pound cake or cinnamon coffee cake, along with a coffee refill.

Though no one had ever bothered his belongings, Dan always tried to claim one of the small tables in a line of sight with the counter, so he could stop worrying about his laptop or his tablet "walking off" in a few seconds left unguarded. At 4 PM, the coffee shop was relatively quiet, with no one manning the cash register, but he knew someone would come to it soon. He took the five steps to the counter and waited.

He saw Sean, the café manager, back by the drip coffee maker. Sean nodded to him and said, "Someone will be with you soon, sir!"

"No problem!" he said. "I'm not in a rush."

Two women entered the back door chatting and carrying shopping bags. Dan leaned on the counter in front of the cash register and perused the offerings in the pastry display case.

The two women walked to the counter ahead of him, still chattering. At that exact moment, a new barista approached the register. She said to the two women, "Can I get something for you?"

Without looking at Dan, one of them said, "We would like to get two large lattes and two blueberry muffins."

Dan looked sideways at them, but they ignored him. The barista rang up the order, took their cash, then turned to Dan as the women walked away, oblivious of anything around them as they continued their conversation.

"And what can I get for you?"

Dan smiled and said, "They didn't even notice I was standing here, did they?"

The barista's smile vanished, and her eyes widened. "Oh! Were you here first? I'm sorry! I didn't mean to let them cut in front of you."

Dan chuckled and waved it off. "It's no problem, and not your fault. I didn't want to say anything. They may have done it on purpose, but probably they just didn't notice, and it wasn't worth making a scene. I just think it's funny."

She smiled again, relieved, and said, "Thank you for understanding! It's hard to keep track of people, even when we're not terribly busy."

Dan pointed to a slice of the iced lemon loaf, and took it back to his table, the incident forgotten.

"That was interesting." The warm contralto seemed to come out of the air a few feet behind him. He looked up to find Callie standing next to his table, smiling softly. She carried a busser tub with a dish towel draped over one shoulder, but she looked calm and relaxed, in no hurry at all.

"Oh, hi, Callie! What was interesting?"

"The way you handled that. A lot of people would have been upset at someone jumping line like that. Why didn't you say anything?"

Callie's manner of asking struck Dan. He often reminded clients that questioning didn't imply doubting or arguing, something people often seemed to assume. Questioning just means inquiring, and Callie's body language communicated no judgment or resistance, only curiosity and openness.

"I thought about it," he said, "but then I thought they were probably lost in conversation and just not noticing what was going on around them. I'll probably never see them again. I couldn't see anything useful resulting from pointing out their rudeness. Besides, they could have gotten defensive. I'll let someone else raise their consciousness."

Callie laughed, and then said, "Have you ever noticed most people seem to go through life unaware of anyone else around them?"

"Now that you mention it, I've often thought that caused most traffic problems. People drive as if there is no one else on the road. They either ignore everyone else or treat them as obstacles."

She nodded thoughtfully and said, "It's almost like, when we grow up, we quit looking around at the rest of the world. It's different for a three-year-old. Isn't it wonderful how they look at everything as if they're seeing it for the first time? Maybe that's because they are!"

"That's pretty wise," Dan said. "I guess in a lot of ways, the average three-year-old is wiser than most adults. They're just so open!"

"Sounds like you're onto something," Callie said. "Maybe you should write that down. Who knows, that could become a speech for you sometime?"

With that, she gave a confident nod and turned away, stopping to pick up some empty mugs left on a table right beside the "please bus your table" sign, giving the table a quick wipe with her towel before disappearing into the kitchen.

I wonder how old she is, thought Dan. Callie could be his daughter, or even his granddaughter, but she seemed confident beyond her years. He realized he really couldn't tell about her age. After teaching college for 40 years, he had learned to recognize students straight out of high school as "typical" college-aged students compared with "non-traditional" students coming back to college.

Straight-from-high-school students looked wide-eyed, lost, and out of their element. Even the ones who swaggered around projected more of an attempt at confidence than actual confidence.

Older students coming back to school after spending time in the workplace sometimes possessed even less confidence. But they usually gave off more of an air of genuine, quiet confidence, especially those breaking out of a familiar pattern to go back to college in their 40s or 50s. Life has a way of making you aware of your limitations and your strengths, and non-traditional students often brought that awareness into the new adventure of mid-life formal education.

Callie exuded the confidence and life experience of one of those older students, but looked as if she could be anywhere between 20 and 40.

Dan gathered his materials to head home. The email could wait until tomorrow, and besides, no doubt Grace needed something done around the house. He needed to get his own work done, but he also didn't want to leave Grace without support any longer than necessary.

Among the papers, he found the receipt from his most recent order nearly an hour ago, well before the incident with the clueless pair. Written on the back in elegant handwriting, he saw:

Like a three-year-old, look for the wonder.

He looked up, but Callie had vanished. Had she written that while she stood talking with him? He hadn't seen it. Had she written it when he picked up his first coffee of the day? But how could she have known they would have a conversation about how three-year-olds handle life? Besides, a different barista had taken his order and handed him the receipt.

Dan thought about what she had said and the note someone had left on the receipt. He tucked the note away, then pulled out the red sketchbook he used for mind mapping and rough outlining. He paused for a moment and then wrote at the top of a blank page.

THE WAY OF THREE-YEAR-OLD WISDOM

He thought a minute more and then jotted down:

The first guideline: Look for the curiosity. Look at the world the way a three-year-old does, as if everything is new. Honor your wonder.

Even curiosity about yourself, Dan thought.

Chapter Three

The Second Three-Year-Old Guideline

Saturday, May 20

"Oh, Hunnee, Ah'm home!" Dan called as he came through the front door in his bad Ricky Ricardo imitation. In the bedroom Grace rolled her eyes, but smiled, though he could see neither. In their 30 years together, despite all the challenges with Hope and health and uncertain income, some things were predictable. That included the silly greeting from the front door that Dan had never tired of. Grace pretended his puns and lame jokes left her groaning. Ten years into their marriage they had irritated her the way fingernails on a chalkboard do, and she had to work to love him despite the annoyance. Now it reminded her of their deep love.

"I'm in here!" she called, as if she would be anywhere else. That, too, had become a ritual, though only in recent years.

Dan appeared in the doorway, holding a box behind him. "Close your eyes and hold out your hands!"

She squinched her eyes shut tight and held her hands out. Before opening them again, she felt all around the cardboard box he handed her, exploring its texture, feeling the tape and the address label. She opened her eyes, looked surprised, and said, "It's a box!"

"Of course it's a box, silly! Open it!"

Dan always opened packages with great care, as if he intended to reuse the box and even the tape, but Grace's enthusiasm moved faster. She cut right through the packaging tape with scissors and began removing bubble wrap and instructional material. Finally, she held up the prize.

"A graphics tablet?!?"

"And a pen with three nibs and a cable to hook it to your computer. I got the padded grip for the pen, too, to help with your arthritis. I know you would rather draw or paint than use the trackball, so I thought this might help."

"When did you get this?"

"Remember when I left to go get the mail yesterday after Hope came out of surgery? I knew this had arrived, and I wanted to surprise you with it."

She held the pad in one hand and the pen in the other, squealed, and said, "Come here for a hug!"

Dan crawled up on the bed and hugged her as best he could without tipping them both over. She smiled at him, and then said, "Now get me my laptop! I have some drawing to do!"

She began humming to herself in happiness, reading the instructions while Dan set up her bed table.

"I'm going to run to the BB to work a bit, if that's OK," he said.

"Sure! I have a ton of stuff to get out of my head, and this will keep me busy for a while."

He quietly closed the door behind him as Grace plugged cables, her isolation for the moment forgotten.

***

Not again, Dan thought. *It's always something.* He scanned the email with the subject line, "Sorry to cancel," then read it more slowly. They had canceled the Zoom workshop on Friday because of an urgent "all hands" company problem. Apologies, etc., and could we reschedule?

Dan sighed. One more situation out of his control but affecting his income. Time to brainstorm some opportunities. He pulled out his red sketchpad and pen, wrote "prospects" in a circle in the middle of a page, and started thinking about people he knew who might need a workshop for their managers.

"Problem?"

Dan recognized Callie's contralto behind him, but he hadn't seen her approach. She never startled him, but he never saw her until she said something. How did she do that? He guessed his work so captivated him that he didn't notice people around him.

"Yeah, just had a gig fall through. It wasn't a large fee, but every bit helps these days. It just makes it hard to predict income, but I guess every small business has that issue."

"Do you mind if I sit down? I'm not starting work for a few minutes."

"Sure, pull up a chair. What's on your mind?"

She pulled one of the beaten-up wooden chairs around to the side of his table and propped her chin on her fist. "I'm interested in the creative process, so I just wondered how you got started with speaking?" Dan noticed a script tattoo in Greek on the inside of her right wrist: ποίησις. Remembering his brief foray into Koine Greek, he thought, *Poiesis. Making or creating something. That really fits.*

"Are you thinking of pursuing speaking?"

She smiled. "Maybe. I've had some pretty good training in the craft already, but I'm just curious about all sorts of creativity. I don't know of too many speakers who set as a life goal becoming a speaker."

"For sure, I never intended to be a speaker," he said. He put down his sketchpad and pen, looked up at the ceiling as if his memories played on a screen up there and smiled. "I actually won the first speech contest I ever entered, back in college."

"Really?" she said. "That's impressive."

"Not really," he said. "I entered the after-dinner-speaking category, and I was the only contestant."

They laughed together, then Dan continued. "The win meant little, but the experience showed me I could enjoy speaking. Even then, I experienced what other people called stage fright as energy. I took every opportunity after that. Other people rode roller coasters or went to scary movies to get a thrill. I spoke."

Callie rubbed her chin, her eyebrows coming together in thought. "If you hadn't intended to be a speaker, why did you enter that contest to begin with?"

Dan smiled. "I intended to work in journalism—started working at a newspaper when I was 14 years old and wrote my first fiction stories when I was 11 or 12. I loved reading, and I loved writing. All my English teachers, especially Mrs. Fortner in high school, encouraged me to write. Journalism was a way to make a living, of sorts, with writing. But the little liberal arts college I went to didn't have a journalism major, just a general communication major. It was the closest I could get. So I received solid training in journalism and writing, but I also had to dig into interpersonal communication, small group communication, public speaking, communication theory, and all kinds of related academic stuff."

He leaned in, as if sharing something in confidence. "Oddly, my English professor ran the contest, not my speech professor. I still don't know for sure what that might mean."

Callie chuckled again. "So, why did you end up speaking instead of writing?"

"It's a long story."

"I'm on my break. How about if I get us fresh coffee and pull up a chair?"

Never one to turn down coffee, Dan readily agreed. He had hit a dead end on his marketing anyway, and he knew he needed to walk away from it for a while.

Callie returned carrying steaming mugs of coffee featuring the Blissful Bean logo, hers filled with jet black brew and Dan's sweetened with plenty of cream and a shot of vanilla, just as he liked.

"How do you know how customers like their coffee?" he asked. "Most people tart up their own except for the shot of flavor."

"You're not customers to me—or at least, not *just* customers," she said. "You're friends—people I care about. I just notice what people do with their coffee after I serve it to them. For me, it's almost like serving communion."

"Interesting. You know, one of my frequent sayings is, 'Connection before content. It doesn't mean the content doesn't matter. It means that without the connection, the content won't matter.' I think you embody that concept."

"Thanks!" she said. "Now about that 'why speaking instead of writing' thing...."

"Right. Well, that's a good question, with layers of answers. The two go together well. Speakers learn that writing a book is a great way for them to market their speaking. Writers, especially authors, learn that speaking is a great way to market their books. Speaking is also a great way to build other kinds of businesses. It's one of the most effective ways of drawing attention to your accounting service, law practice, consulting service, you name it. Heck, one of the highest-paid and best-known professional speakers got started by using speaking to build her hair-dressing business!"

"Hair dressing! That's certainly a creative business, but you rarely associate it with speaking."

"She learned to tell stories in making conversation with clients while they say in her chair, and expanded from there. Back in the early 90s, I started speaking because there was some demand for my topic, and it could lead to an immediate paycheck. I wrote regularly for a business publication, which led to a steady paycheck, but other kinds of writing often had a long lead time. Before the Internet, a lot of freelance writing happened through old-fashioned postal mail—you probably don't remember that."

"It might surprise you what I remember! Let's just say I understand the concept. But tell me how you actually worked then."

"I wrote a lot for small special-interest and regional magazines. The process involved sending a query letter to an editor, waiting a few weeks for a response, doing the research, writing the piece, mailing it in, waiting for it to be published in a few months, and then waiting another month or two for the check to come in the mail. But I found out that I could speak and get paid almost immediately."

Dan shook his head, then continued. "There were still delays—most companies and associations would contract with a speaker six months or even a year ahead of time. But I could ask for a deposit up front to 'hold the date.' And I could get paid within 30 days of giving the speech. Sometimes they would hand me a check right then!"

Callie took a sip, looked thoughtful, and said, "So it was just driven by economics?"

"Not entirely. I enjoyed the energy of getting up on stage, the feeling that came when I saw the 'light bulbs' go on for audience members, when I would see them engaged with the material and know I was making a difference."

"Was it always like that, that feeling?"

"Oh, no! Sometimes what usually felt like energy felt like fear. I think that's what many people experience when they label it 'stage fright.' At those times, I would ask myself why I ever consider speaking a good idea, and I would vow never to do it again. Other times, I just could *not* connect with the audience."

Dan smiled at a memory playing back in his mind. "Once I spoke for an in-service at a high school, presenting powerful ideas for engaging with students, and ironically having trouble reaching them. The coaches attended only because the principal required it. They all sat in the back two rows and read newspapers and chatted the whole time I talked! Those times made me want to give up. But most of the time I got such a charge out of speaking that I would have done it for free."

Callie looked directly in his eyes and said, "Do you still get that feeling?"

There was a long pause. Dan started to speak, but then Callie said, "Oops! I've overstayed my break. Gotta run! Thanks for the visit! We'll talk more later."

She gathered the empty cups and headed off behind the counter. Before disappearing around the corner, she turned and said, "I gotta wonder, though. Even if you still get that feeling, is it different from the feeling you get from writing?"

He blinked, and she was gone, leaving Dan to wonder by himself.

***

His cell phone chimed, signaling a text from Grace. "Pick up Hope's meds on the way home? And Liana needs to leave a little early, so could you come on home? Please?"

He looked at the time on the screen, realized the coffee shop would close soon, and soon after, the pharmacy would as well. It looked as if brainstorming prospects would have to wait.

This wasn't the first time he had to stop work to step in when a nurse suddenly needed to take care of something at their own home. He knew he needed to pack up soon, but he also needed to think a bit. He pulled out his sketchbook, turned to a fresh page, and wrote "Charge out of speaking?" in the middle. Ideas flowed quickly, surfacing a variety of experiences over the years. After only about three minutes, he paused and looked over the whole page. He focused on one particular leg that helped him realize when the spark had gone out of speaking for him. He lost it about the time Hope spent three long weeks in the hospital fighting off RSV when she was about 15.

Respiratory syncytial virus. What a mouthful! Dan had never heard of it, but when Hope's lungs started filling up like tubs with jello, he learned a lot quickly. In adults, RSV might cause a common cold, but in the elderly and infants, it can quickly lead to pneumonia and death. Most teenagers would have moved beyond the danger zone, but Hope's special needs left her as vulnerable as any infant.

The movie of his memory took him back to one particular night during that stay. RSV patients filled half the hospital rooms, and an aura of anxiety surrounded the entire building. Bleary, red-eyed parents wandered the halls at all hours, taking advantage of the free coffee on each floor to them to help them stay awake for their children.

As Dan walked through the hall on the way to Hope's room, he could glimpse through open doors parents, siblings, whole families gathered around small beds and cribs, murmuring among themselves. Every cluster surrounded a frail, still figure in the middle. Pulse-oximeters beeped everywhere, with many of them "singing the song of their people" as one respiratory tech called the low-oxygen alarms, and nurses scrambled to deal with them all.

When he reached Hope's room, he found a doctor, a nurse he didn't recognize, and the hospital chaplain along with Grace. Back then, Hope still moved occasionally, turning her head to follow a voice or pulling her arm away when a phlebotomist tried once again to find a vein that had not been so scarred by IVs as to be unusable. Today, she lay still as a sack of sand, unresponsive to anything going on in the room.

"Mr. Roberts, I know this is a hard conversation to have," the unfamiliar nurse said. "And we're certainly not giving up hope. But we think it might be a good time for us to talk a little about... well, about whether, if it comes down to it, whether you and Mrs. Roberts would want to donate any of Hope's organs."

She talked more, but Dan didn't really hear her, couldn't hear her. He looked over at Grace, teary-eyed, saying nothing, looking right back at him. He took Hope's hand, the one without the IV in the back, and squeezed it, though he received no squeeze back.

They had talked before about the need to be realistic about Hope's chances, about the likelihood that at some point her condition would no longer be "compatible with life" in the cold, clinical terminology they had heard since her birth. Twice before, they had thought she had reached that stage. But it had never felt so imminent.

The rest of that night blurred into fog, but he remembered the empty, hollow feeling in his chest that acted as a drain for concern about anything other than keeping his daughter alive. He kept working, of course. They still needed to pay the bills. They also needed to keep the insurance that provided quality medical care beyond the minimum that state Medicaid would provide. But they also needed to avoid earning more than what would qualify her for state Medicaid. Hope's primary insurance did not cover the home nursing care that kept her protected from infections in hospital rooms full of other children.

In other words, to keep the coverage necessary for Hope's survival, the state prohibited Dan from practicing financial responsibility, like earning more money and growing savings. Dan kept pursuing speaking gigs because that's what he did, but his heart was no longer in it.

He shook his head to clear it, remembered he had to get to the pharmacy before it closed. As much as he disliked the disruptions to his schedule, memories of worse times made him grateful he could still have such disruptions. The only way to have complete control over his time involved a loss he didn't want to contemplate.

As he closed up his laptop, he picked up the receipt for his coffee, paused, and checked the back. No note today. Slightly disappointed, he kept packing, then gathered the trash. As he started to toss the napkins and such in the garbage, he noticed a brightly colored note card between two of them.

Pulling it out, he saw a crayon drawing of a chicken on the front. He opened the note, which said, "Why did the chicken cross the road? To get to the other side. But nobody ever asks why the chicken wanted to cross the road. Did he have hungry chicks over there? Was he being chased by Colonel Sanders? The rest of the sentence says, 'To get to the other side *so that*....' You may have noticed three-year-olds keep asking why. Look for the 'so that.'"

No signature, but the same elegant handwriting as the previous note.

Dan looked around, but saw no one else around this close to closing time except for Jim, who was always there sipping coffee and reading an ever-present book. Jim looked up and nodded in recognition, then went back to reading.

He hadn't seen the note earlier among the napkins. When did it show up? If it hadn't come from Callie, the note writer must have overheard their conversation on Wednesday. Maybe Jim? If so, the handwriting certainly didn't fit, although appearances deceive.

Dan pulled out his red sketchbook and turned to the page where he had written the first guideline.

He wrote:

The second guideline: Look for the "so that." A three-year-old doesn't stop with the first answer. He still wants to know "why." What's the outcome?

Is paying the bills enough "so that"? Dan thought. It would have to wait. Right now, he had a date at the pharmacy.

Chapter Four

The Third Three-Year-Old Guideline

Monday, May 22

The Blissful Bean made getting the house blend easy. If you brought your own mug, you could drop two dollars in the bucket by the row of airpots with the day's brews and draw your own. But Dan preferred four shots of vanilla in his coffee, so he always stood in line.

Today, no one else stood in line, a rarity, so he went straight to the cash register to find Callie behind it.

"Hi, Dan!" She almost glowed, genuine warmth with no veneer. Staff tended to not wear name tags, but he remembered Callie's name, and it impressed him that she remembered his. *Maybe she does that with all the regular customers,* he thought, although he seldom saw her at the cash register. He thought she mostly concocted special brews, while others took care of orders. Still, it was nice to be recognized.

"Hi back, Callie! You're very energetic for a Monday morning!"

"How could you not get energized working at The Blissful Bean?" she said. "I'm surrounded by caffeine. Of course, it's the people who keep me energized. Like, I enjoyed hearing about your start in the speaking business. I've done a bit of that myself."

"Oh, really? What topics?"

"Different topics, depending on what the audience needed to hear," she said. "Mostly small audiences. Sometimes audiences of one." She laughed, a sound like a melody but unselfconscious.

"But our last conversation left me wondering. You told me how you got into speaking, and I heard all the reasons you stuck with it. But it felt like maybe there was something missing. You seemed to spark up when you talked about writing in your early days. Can you tell me a little more about that period?"

Dan looked quizzical, and she said, "I'm interested in writing, too. I'm more interested in epic poetry and that sort of thing, but I love all sorts of writing. Just wondering."

Dan checked behind him and saw no one there. In fact, the entire coffee shop had gone quiet, as if just the two of them stood at the cash register conversing. *As long as I'm not holding anyone up....*

"I have to admit, it was magical," he said. "I didn't like school in the early days and spent a lot of time in the principal's office. I hated the stuff they forced you to read, making it just a chore. But then I discovered in sixth grade you could have fun reading books nobody made you read. Who knew?"

They both chuckled at that. "Do you remember those first books?" she asked.

"I can tell you exactly the first one. Our little town had a hole-in-the-wall public library, and I wandered in there one day. For some reason, I pulled *Have Spacesuit, Will Travel* by Robert A. Heinlein off the shelf. Read it straight through in one afternoon. Heinlein amazed me with the way he could put me right in a scene and make me hear his characters in my head. I returned that one and checked out another of his, *Podkayne of Mars*. Then *Red Planet*. Then *Starship Troopers*."

"Wow," she said, "you remember those specific titles after all these years?"

"Are you implying I'm old?" he smiled, and she smiled back without embarrassment. "I can't tell you every book I've read, but I remember those first ones. I read every Heinlein book they had, and then Isaac Asimov, Harlan Ellison, Jerry Pournelle, E.E. 'Doc' Smith, Ray Bradbury, and others. Eventually, I thought, 'I'd sure like to do that.'"

As Dan talked, Callie noticed him standing straighter, looking off into the distance of his memory, and smiling softly. She kept quiet and listened.

"That's when I wrote those first stories. I have them tucked away somewhere. Written in longhand in pencil, they're hard to read—the pencil has faded, but they're also so bad! I had no clue about plotting. Sometimes I just wrote about characters doing things I wanted to do, traveling in space, making friends, and so forth. But they didn't actually do anything. I guess it was like Seinfeld years before he was cool. I didn't want to cause trouble for the characters—just wanted them happy."

Dan laughed to himself, remembering those early efforts. "Of course, any writer knows you have to put your characters in difficult circumstances. Otherwise, nobody will care about them. So eventually, I learned to, as one writer said, 'get my characters up a tree and throw rocks at them.' But then I couldn't figure out how to get them out of the tree. More than once, I wrote something like, 'and then the ship blew up. The end.' Lame."

This time, Callie laughed along with him.

"I ran into the editor of our little hometown newspaper on the sidelines of the high school football games. He let me hang around the office, running errands, fetching coffee and such, and he put up with my questions. Some time later, he let me write a story—an obituary, if I remember correctly. I must have done all right, because he let me write a news story, then another one, and then another.

"Eventually, I needed to actually earn some money for gasoline and dating and other high school stuff. When I told him I was leaving to take a job driving a delivery truck, he started paying me to keep me around."

"You must have been doing OK as a writer for him to want to keep you."

"You want to know the truth?" Dan looked right and left, then leaned over and whispered conspiratorially. "I think I worked cheap and provided him with copy to fill the paper. It wasn't exactly Pulitzer Prize material. Most of the stories concerned city council meetings, church potlucks, and community events. But I started getting a feel for words on paper. And when I say 'feel,' I mean *feel*. When language is right, you can tell that it just *fits*, the way a properly sized hat just *fits*."

He paused, closed his eyes, and said, "I've never been able to describe it any other way. I'm supposed to be handy with words, but I'm at a loss to come up with a better description of what writing is for me—always has been, and still is. It felt that way with those silly little 12-year-old stories, and it feels that way now even when I write marketing copy. I love speaking, don't get me wrong. But there's something different for me about writing."

The man in line behind him said, "That sounds really cool!"

Dan, startled, looked around for Callie before realizing she had slipped away. The guy smiled at him, and the woman behind him peered around to add her smile.

Dan blushed, then grabbed his cup with four shots of vanilla and headed to the "fill your own" station. The guy behind him turned to the woman and said, "It's kind of cool to hear people talking about the things they care about."

"Who was he talking to?" she said.

"I think he must have been on the phone. You can never tell with earbuds these days."

***

"I hate my hands!" Dan heard as he came in the front door. *Uh-oh*, he thought. *I'd better not give a cheery greeting today.* Grace hadn't expected him home yet, but he had come home to grab the headphones he had forgotten that afternoon. He hesitantly opened the bedroom door and poked his head in. "Safe to come in?" he asked. "How have your hands offended you?"

Grace sat upright in the bed, her laptop open on one side on the little bed table and her new graphics tablet on her lap. She had her arms crossed and her hands tucked into her armpits. Her face displayed something between a frown and a pout.

"They just won't work!"

"I know what you mean. I can never get my hands to do what my brain wants them to."

"You've never been able to! I once could, but I can't any more!"

Dan looked hurt, and Grace immediately said, "I'm sorry. I didn't mean it to sound so bad, but I'm soooooo frustrated!"

"I know," he said, "and you're right, it's not the same thing. Do you think something's wrong with the tablet?"

"No, the tablet's fine. It's taking exactly what I'm giving it, but I just can't draw like I used to."

"How long has it been since you drew anything on any medium using a pen or a brush?"

"I don't know. At least five years, I guess."

"And how often did you draw before your arthritis got so bad?"

"Probably every day," she said. Tool boxes, draft tables, stacks of sketchpads, canvases, framed finished paintings, raw charcoal drawings, and half-finished pen-and-ink pieces filled Grace's craft room. Her arthritis had hit suddenly, like an Arizona thunderstorm, interrupting multiple projects.

"Do you think that maybe, just maybe, you're rusty?"

Grace once again crossed her arms and tucked her hands, but looked decidedly angry this time. "I don't know. Maybe."

"So, give it time. Maybe if you keep at it, you'll regain enough dexterity to at least be a slightly satisfying."

She said nothing more, so Dan turned and went to his home office for the headphones. When the door shut, Grace mumbled, "Sometimes I just want you to listen, not fix it."

But he's right, she thought. Despite the gap between the picture she held in her mind and that on the computer screen, drawing again, or at least the attempt, felt good. The "feel good" outweighed the "hurts bad" in her hands. She sighed, cleared the screen, and started over.

***

Dan took his coffee and retrieved headphones back to the table where he had set up his laptop, sipping it even though it had grown cold. His mind drifted back to his talk that morning with Callie and those science fiction books of long ago. He had read none of them for several years. Modern science fiction didn't hold his attention. Mainly, though, he thought he didn't have time to read.

Only weeks before, he and Grace had made a trip to a Barnes and Noble store in a nearby city, the first time they'd been in a physical bookstore in a couple of years. Since Hope had arrived in their lives,

Dan found it harder and harder to read—hard to focus for any length of time since her care required frequent interruptions. Even after they had jumped through all the state's hoops to qualify for nursing care for Hope, Grace's increasing challenges had added to the interruptions. Such interruptions robbed him of the ability to concentrate on anything, even fun activities.

Reading had always been his primary enjoyment, second only to the satisfaction of writing. But in the last decade, he couldn't finish reading even a magazine article. Like so many people, he wasted hours on social media, flitting from post to post with each holding his attention just long enough to spark a bit of dopamine to relieve the stresses of daily life, but giving no creative or learning satisfaction.

At least when he worked on a speech or marketing materials he could get slight creative satisfaction in short bursts. He could focus on a three- or four-paragraph email long enough to have some impact before having to, once again, stop and tend to something more urgent, if not more important.

It hadn't happened overnight, but it had happened, the way the mythical frog gets boiled: through slow change.

When was the last time he read something just for fun?

He shook his head, opened up the laptop again, and found a vintage postcard lying on the keyboard.

Yellowed and tattered, someone had addressed it to him, but there was no stamp or postmark. Its front showed a cover for Fantastic Science Fiction magazine from February 1952—probably a reproduction, though the card looked old enough to date from that time. The ink in the address and message appeared faded with age, but the handwriting looked familiar.

The same handwriting that had appeared on the mysterious notes over the last few days.

Dan pulled out his glasses and focused on the message.

"Don't discount emotion, Dan," it read. "Humans are emotional creatures. We're not *just* emotional, but we ignore emotion at our peril. It is one of the most important ways you communicate with yourself. While you shouldn't act on an emotion without thinking about it, you should pay attention. Ask yourself what it means."

No signature. Again.

How had this note wound up tucked in his laptop? Had someone messed with the computer? He checked the screen, but the machine appeared still locked behind its passcode.

This is getting weirder, he thought. But the notes all seemed related and on target somehow.

Dan looked around, but nobody watched him for a reaction to the note.

Not sure what prompted him to do so, he took out his sketchbook, turned to the list he had started, and wrote:

The third guideline: Look for the emotion. A three-year-old mainly responds to emotion, as we all do. He just doesn't hide it. Without emotion, there is no motion.

He considered what he had written and thought, *No motion. I haven't been moving... but I felt moved today.*

Chapter Five

The Fourth Three-Year-Old Guideline

Friday, May 26

It had been almost a week since Dan had made it to The Blissful Bean. Every day, it seemed, he meant to take time to go there so he could focus on marketing and contact emails, but then a doctor would call or Grace would need him to run to the bank or something else would lead him to put it off "until tomorrow."

But today Dan insisted on the trip to the coffee shop. Partly, he needed the concentration time. He also needed to pull together the proposal for Elizabeth Martinez by the Monday deadline if he was going to have a chance at that gig.

Mainly, though, he needed time to think. The mystery of the notes kept coming to mind as he plowed through laundry; the conversations with Callie replayed in his mind as well. He thought about what those interactions had surfaced, but then something else demanded his attention and he moved the thoughts onto the back shelf of his brain.

He really needed to focus on the proposal. But he kept coming back to the Callie talks, and he decided he needed to figure some things out *now*. So Dan took time for himself, just him, his laptop, and his sketchbook.

Dan went through the ordering line at The BB and grabbed his usual coffee plus a blueberry scone. As he laid out his favorite pen and turned to a fresh page for some mind mapping, a familiar voice, like a familiar song, sounded in his ear.

"Doing a little writing?" Callie asked.

Dan turned to her and smiled. "Of sorts," he said.

"Working on a speech?"

"Not this time," he said. "Today is just for me. You've helped me realize in our conversations that writing is a pretty special part of who I am, but you also reminded me I've always used writing as a thinking tool. Writing is thinking, you know. Joan Didion once said, 'I write entirely to find out what I'm thinking,' and lots of other people have said something similar. That's certainly the case for me."

"Interesting. I once had a teacher who said a complete sentence was the basic unit of thought. It's almost like you don't really have a thought until you can put words to it."

"Your teacher sounds pretty wise."

"So what are you thinking about through your writing today?"

"I don't know yet," he smiled. "I haven't written yet. But you've certainly given me a lot to think about."

Dan paused, then said, "I don't mean to pry, but I don't have a clue as to… well, how old are you? No offense, and I don't mean to pry, so feel welcome to tell me it's none of my business. But you seem wise beyond your apparent years. Are you a college student somewhere around here?"

"I appreciate that! But let's just say I'm well beyond college age. However, I have found that learning never stops. Wouldn't you agree?"

"I used to think that," Dan said. "I've always believed lifelong learning should be the default, but I'm not sure I've really learned anything the last few years. I've just been repeating things I've already learned. But lately, I've been getting some nudges toward at least a different way of looking at things, and I suppose that's learning too."

"Nudges?"

"You're part of it. You're not so much telling me things I didn't know as asking questions that lead me to think of things a little differently."

"I'm glad!" she said. "I enjoy prompting people to think. In fact, I have a license for it—sort of goes along with being a barista these days. Like being a bar tender, only in cleaner places."

They chuckled, and Callie reached into her back pocket and pulled out a worn wallet made of thick, durable leather. Dark brown with surface flecks missing, it seemed both ancient and timeless. A strap of the same material wrapped around it, securing it shut. Callie unfastened the strap and fished into one of the many pockets before producing a card and handing it to Dan.

The card looked liked old papyrus, laminated with no sign of a single scratch but slightly bent to conform to the curve of the wallet. At the top in official-looking script it read, "License to Ask." It said that the bearer was entitled to ask thoughtful questions in the service of understanding and inspiration. He couldn't quite read the signature (though he noted with disappointment that it appeared to be a different hand than the one that penned his mystery messages), but he could see the license had been issued to Calliope Anagnostopoulos.

"See?" she said. "I'm entitled. Says so right there." She smiled and returned the card to the ancient wallet that disappeared into a pocket that couldn't possibly hold it.

"So here's a question for you before I have to get back to making magic potions from beans: Most people can name someone in their past whose support made an enormous difference in their life choices. Who was it for you?"

"That's easy," said Dan. "My dad was always my greatest supporter. It was like he was proud of everything I did, whatever it was. Mom too, but she was always more worried about me being secure. She wanted me to get a civil service job. Back then, if you had a government job, you would have to get caught selling drugs to your supervisor and then murdering him with a chainsaw to get fired.

"Dad never finished high school, but he fully supported me in pursuing every educational endeavor. I think he was more comfortable with me teaching college for a living, since he saw that as being fairly secure. But he also supported my writing and speaking, though he didn't really understand how you could make a living at that."

"Was he proud of what you were doing?"

"Oh, yeah. I remember coming home for a visit one time. Dad was out in the kitchen cooking up some stuff, and I was poking through the old house. They had turned my old bedroom into a sort of office—you know, a place to store papers and pay the bills, that sort of thing, though some of my things remained stacked in the closet. I noticed a scrapbook on the desk, and when I looked in it I found clippings of every newspaper story I had ever written and clippings about speeches I gave to businesses and associations."

Dan looked down at his hands for a moment, lost in memory, before continuing.

"The thing that struck me was that some of those clippings came from little newspapers in other towns, or company newsletters—not the kind of thing you would pick up at a newsstand in my hometown. How he got ahold of those things, I don't know, but he had gone to some trouble to gather a record of those achievements. He never said much about it. Dad was a man of few words. But that told me how proud he was of what I was doing."

"That's a great story," Callie said. "Have you ever written that one down somewhere?"

"Now that you mention it... I probably should. It's funny, but I've never stuck with keeping a journal or anything like that. That's one of those things that fell through the cracks because it didn't directly make me any money. But I should write down those memories, if for no other reasons than to pass them down."

"Well, I'm glad he let you know how proud he is of you."

"Was, I'm afraid. Unfortunately, he died nearly 20 years ago."

"I'm sorry you can't talk with him anymore, but when I said 'is,' that's what I meant." Her smile took any sting out of her words, and Dan smiled back.

"I like that thought. Thank you."

"My pleasure. Too often we don't tell each other things like that. We think people just know, but they don't know unless we tell them. Which reminds me: I'll bet you're proud of Grace's art work, right?"

"Oh, absolutely! I'm amazed at what she used to do, and even now she has more creativity in an eyelash that I have in my whole body."

"Does *she* know you think that of her?"

"Well.... I *think* she does. I know I've told her. I just don't know if she believes me. I think she probably has an advanced case of imposter syndrome. I'm not sure what to do to convince her."

Callie smiled again. "Would you like a suggestion?"

"Please!"

"I'm sure you've noticed that we have a regular showing of area artists that we display on our walls here."

Dan looked around at the current offerings by a variety of local artists. He always looked at the new exhibits when they went up.

"Absolutely. I'll tell you honestly, sometimes I look at them and think, 'Grace could draw circles around some of these folks.' Figuratively, of course."

"So, have you thought about how people get those things exhibited? They don't just waltz in here and hang them. How do you think Grace would react if you talked to Sean about exhibiting her prints? I understand she's done some really impressive work since you got her that graphic tablet."

Dan couldn't remember updating Callie on what Grace had accomplished—he hadn't seen her work himself that he could recall, but he must have. He thought about it for just a couple of seconds, and then said, "That's a wonderful idea! She might resist doing it, but I think it would signal that I believe in her, even if Sean doesn't bite."

"Perfect! You know, his office is right upstairs. If you can get a few shots of her work on your phone, you could easily show him what she can do. Whether you do that, I'm hoping you will write down those stories about your dad. As you said, at least a way of preserving the memory."

"Good point. I may use that story in a speech sometime. It has all the marks of a good story rather than a lecture on a principle."

"Once upon a time, right?" she said. "Well, once upon a time I needed to get back to making coffee, and that time is now. Happy writing!"

And with that, she was gone again.

***

Grace's hands trembled a little, and not from the arthritis. Digital art was one thing. Making hard copies and showing them to the world was another. Paying hard-earned cash to make high-quality prints really crossed into the land of serious.

Dan knew more about printing than she did—after all, he had worked in a print shop back in his college days. But printing had changed since then, and besides, this needed a different sort of printing than the mass production he had done.

Grace wanted prime quality output on heavy paper or even canvas, something she could add paint or other material to in order to build up a three-dimensional effect. In her own college days, she would have sought a silk screen printer. Now, she had no idea what she needed, just a clear idea of the outcome she wanted.

And that she needed to take care of it herself.

She trusted Dan, but this was her baby. Besides, the man had a way with words, but he didn't understand color, design, or visual appeal. He joked that as a man, he could only see six colors.

Grace thought it more likely he could only see four. And while he would understand the technicalities of whatever printing process she settled on, he would not speak the artistic lingo an art printmaker would instinctively understand.

No, this was not only something she needed to do herself. It was something she *could* do herself. Thanks to the wonders of the Internet and the telephone system, she could take care of every bit up to picking up the finished work and hanging the prints.

Besides, Dan had already contributed a lot. So much had happened today already!

He had come back from The BB all excited, said he had a surprise for her.

"First, let me give you a context," he said. She readied herself to let him ramble, since he often ran ideas by her in a sort of "thinking out loud" that had nothing to do with her. She loved that he trusted her that way, and she also secretly loved that she could keep working on her artwork while he talked.

He started talking about a barista who had helped him think about writing again, about what mattered most to him beyond Grace and Hope.

He said the barista (Callie? That seemed to be her name) had suggested he talk with The BB manager about hanging her artwork in the shop exhibit, and he had done so, and Sean had seen her work on Dan's phone, and....

"Wait a minute," Grace had said. The conversation had suddenly centered on her, and it took a moment for her to shift her concentration. "You showed somebody my work? I didn't even know you had copies on your phone."

"You sent them to me, remember? I asked you how the tablet was working out, and you sent me JPEGs. I held onto them. Normally I wouldn't show them to anyone else without asking you, because they're yours, not mine, but this ... this was such an opportunity, hon! I'm sorry if this upsets you. I'm just proud of your work, and I know you do such good work, and I want the world to know it, and.... Did I screw up?"

"I ... I don't know what to say! I'm not mad, I'm just surprised. He really thought he wanted to hang my stuff? Did you twist his arm or something?"

"Not at all! I think maybe he looked at them just to humor a steady customer, but I could see his eyes light up as soon as he looked at my phone. He took it out of my hands, scrolled through the gallery, and said, 'You know, we were looking for the next exhibitor. I think we just found her!'"

Grace went from elation to "Oh, God, what do I do now?" in about two seconds. She shooed Dan out of the room ("Go away, now, I have to think!") and just sat for a while. She opened her laptop, scrolled through the creations she had made for herself since Dan had brought her the tablet. As she looked at each one, she considered how it would look on the wall of the coffee shop.

Almost without conscious decision, she Googled "local print shops and printmakers." Her hands trembled. But, by George, she dialed.

* * *

Friday night meant spending time with Hope, since they had no nurse for the evening. *Good thing that gig fell through*, thought Dan. Otherwise, he would have once again found himself "between a rock and a hard place," as his mother used to say.

He hated missing the speaking opportunity. But Dan looked forward to quiet time with Hope. She needed a lot of attention since she could have back-to-back seizures or choke on her own saliva, but she couldn't argue or fight or engage in any other "difficult" teenage angsty behaviors. While her care was demanding, Hope herself was not.

He sometimes wished Hope gave him the same challenges her siblings had when they went through adolescence. He often saw parents dealing with toddler antics in a store or overheard conversations of other parents concerned with their teenagers activities, and he wanted to say to them, "Be grateful. Be glad they can give you trouble, because they'll come out of it on the other side, and you will all be better for the struggle." But he knew he would not have been receptive to such advice before Hope arrived as his greatest teacher, so he kept quiet. Tonight, he valued just sitting with her, holding her hand.

Dan still felt confused by his conversation with Grace, but now he had to concentrate on Hope's care. He got all the details of the report from Kathleen, Hope's Friday day nurse, Number, size, and consistency of bowel movements. Time of the last catheterization. Temperature, blood pressure, pulse rate patterns. Number of seizures. Extra PRN medication administrations and verification of the regular doses of the 27 "normal" meds. Doctor updates to pass on to Liana tomorrow.

Notes taken, he bid Kathleen goodbye and then stood over Hope's bed for a while. If he stood just right, it looked as if she gazed back at him somberly. If he moved to the right or left, though, her focus never shifted, and he questioned if she saw him at all.

"I guess you're as complicated as any teenager, honey. Just in unique ways."

Whenever Dan spent time in Hope's room, he talked with her, even though very little showed she could hear him. She had never in her life uttered a word, but in the early days of her development she would turn toward someone speaking, and her eyes would register interest, amusement, or anger. As time went on, even the hint of apparent interaction ceased, though no one knew if it stemmed from neurological deterioration or the impact of her multiple anti-seizure meds. Still, almost everyone involved in her care talked with her because they had no way of knowing whether she experienced locked-in syndrome.

Dan hated the idea that she might know everything going on around her, could hurt from not being turned frequently enough or itch from a stray hair, but couldn't turn, scratch, or tell anybody else where it hurt or itched. Part of him hoped she had no awareness of her situation or surroundings. Because he knew nothing about her experience, he talked, "just in case," as much as he could manage.

"You know," he said, "I never would have thought I would say this, but I wish you could be as big a pain in the ass as your brothers and sisters were."

Hope slowly closed her eyes, opened them again.

"You ought to be going to dances, and I ought to be intimidating boys wanting to take you to them. We should be looking at college applications. You should be doing your best to extend your curfew."

Dan drew up her 8 PM meds, administered them, and then said, "How about if we read from that new book Mom got for you? I'll read to you and show you the pictures. OK? Now, don't argue!"

Hope never moved, her breathing and pulse steady, blessedly free from seizures. But Dan thought he saw a little spark in her eyes. He got the book from the shelf, pulled up a stool beside her bed, and read to her from *The Boy, the Mole, the Fox and the Horse*, holding the book up in her line of sight with every turn of a page.

Dan read slowly, enunciating each word and attempting to use different voices for each of the four characters. When he reached the end (where the author marked out "The End" and handwrote a better, more hopeful ending), he closed the book and said, "That was quite a story, wasn't it?"

He looked at Hope and saw that she had not moved, of course. But he also noticed that a single tear had escaped her right eye and trickled halfway down toward her ear as she lay on her back. He took one of the ever-present white cloths from the bedside table, wiped away the tear, and suctioned her trach one more time.

***

Saturday, May 27

Dan hadn't bothered to bring his laptop today. With just coffee, pen, and paper, he intended to surface some ideas that had been running through his mind ever since last night in Hope's room.

He wasn't sure whether he had an idea for a speech or a workshop, a blog post or something more. He only knew something floated just under the surface, and he needed to get it (whatever "it" was) out where he could work with it.

Dan turned to a blank sheet in his sketchbook. He had long used mind maps to get started with a speech, rough out a magazine article, solve a problem, or even generate a grocery list. He had invested in all sorts of computer programs and phone apps to not only generate electronic mind maps but also store them, since paper had a way of disappearing. Inevitably, though, he came back to paper and pen. It slowed him down, and that made it more useful—he had to take time with each thought.

In the middle of a page, Dan wrote "Story" and circled it. Then he started letting associations come to him, jotting them down without judging them, drawing circles around the words or just writing on a line, drawing lines to connect ideas in no particular order.

Dan felt the sort of flow that he had learned to allow without interference, something he used to find hard to maintain. A Buddhist psychologist had captured the feeling in the title of his book: *Here I Am, Wasn't I*. It's a delicate balance to recognize you're in the flow without breaking the flow, but mind mapping helped him do that.

With a last circle, Dan felt the familiar sense of "Done!" and he knew he was ready to write. He hadn't finished the thought exploration, not at all, but the next step involved taking the mind map and shaping it into a linear train of thought, figuring out what he thought. If it turned into something he would later develop into a finished piece, it would still need plenty of rewriting and polishing before presenting it to an audience. Now, though, he had preserved ideas before they could evaporate like clouds in a July Texas sky. He could mentally take a step back and find the through-line that would reveal his thinking to himself.

He took the last bite of the scone and reached for a napkin from the dispenser in the center of the big table. As he started to wipe his mouth, he saw something on the napkin out of the corner of his eye.

Writing. Handwriting. On the napkin, he had just pulled from the dispenser.

He pulled another one, then another one, and another one. Plain old napkins, sans writing.

Dan fished his glasses from his pocket and read: "Go beyond emotion, Dan. People have always used stories and storytelling to figure out what an experience means!" He noticed that "means" had been underlined twice. More followed.

"Meaning doesn't exist objectively. Humans *create* (more underlining) meaning, and we usually do so through story. An old dead Greek guy once said, 'It's not what happens to you, but what you think about what happens to you that determines your experience.' What story will you tell?"

Dan picked up the napkin dispenser, looked underneath it, checked the top, not at all sure what he was looking for. He looked around, but no one appeared to watch him.

He was tempted to shout out, "OK, who keeps leaving me these notes?!?" But he didn't want to attract attention or make people think him crazy. Maybe he *was* crazy, after all.

What the heck, he thought. *I've been jotting this stuff down. Might as well keep it up.*

Still glancing around, Dan turned back to the page headed THE WAY OF THREE-YEAR-OLD WISDOM, glanced at the mind map he had torn out, and then wrote:

The fourth guideline: Look for the story. Three-year-olds love stories, just as we all do. A story brings together emotion and reasoning to create meaning. Find the story, create the story, and you will find meaning.

Nobody would believe THIS story, he thought. *And I'm still trying to figure out what it means.*

Chapter Six

The Fifth Three-Year-Old Guideline

Monday, May 29

Dan checked his watch. Only two hours to go until he had promised Elizabeth Martinez an updated proposal focused on a virtual workshop and associated training. Time tightened around him, but he felt confident he could meet the deadline. After all, the material itself came from topics he had presented dozens of times before, and he had had enough conversations with Elizabeth to understand the unique challenges and opportunities within Agile Manufacturing.

Nothing seemed to stand in his way. Except for that dry feeling. *Why can't I just finish this thing?*

THE WAY OF THE THREE-YEAR-OLD WHY

His old friend Don Brown popped into his mind. Don had worked as chief engineer at a radio station where Dan worked as the morning drive DJ and program director. Don told him two kinds of engineers worked in radio.

The first kind wanted to implement routines to keep things running smoothly. Ideally, someone else figured out what needed doing, and the maintenance-oriented engineer would do it efficiently, dependably, and on time.

The second kind loved solving problems, figuring out something never before attempted. They lived for challenges and adrenaline, but got bored with routine maintenance.

Don clearly embodied the second kind. In the early days of personal computers, Don owned a Commodore 64, so named because of its (for the time) large 64-kilobyte memory. Supposedly, that represented the maximum the device could handle. Don had refused to accept that limitation. Before memory sticks, flash drives, or anything resembling them, he had figured out a way to expand the RAM on his Commodore 64 (which he slept with) to a full megabyte. ("That's more than the whole federal government has!" he claimed.)

Dan believed if he asked Don Brown to build a personal fission reactor, Don would do it with parts bought at RadioShack and cobbled from leftover pieces of a radio transmitter. But he wouldn't write any of it down, and he would lose all interest in doing it again.

Maybe I'm a second kind, too, Dan thought. *Or maybe I just get bored too easily.*

"You don't look bored, Dan, but you do look like you're puzzling over something."

Dan turned to find the now familiar Callie holding out a cup of something steaming.

"For me? Thank you! What is it?"

"Try something new. It's called a London Fog—but I sweetened it up the way I know you would like it."

He blew across the frothy top to cool it a bit, took a sip, and said, "Wow! That is good! You read my mind. In fact, I was just thinking I might be bored, and then you told me it was something else. Special ability?"

Again, she smiled. "Not mind reading, just face reading. You're turning something over in there. Problem?"

"I'm not sure it's a problem," he said. He told her about Don Brown, embellishing the memory a bit as they both chuckled over the eccentric genius.

"You used that word twice in your story," Callie said. "Genius. It's an interesting word. The ancient Romans didn't say you *were* a genius. They sais you *had* a genius.

"Really? I did not know. Where did you learn that?"

"Oh, I don't remember. It's something I learned a long time ago. I remember Augustine thought your 'genius' might be the same thing as your soul. It's a little different from, but similar to, the idea of the Muses. Have you heard of them?"

"Only all my life," Dan laughed. "My first editor constantly reminded me I had a deadline, and I had to produce whether or not my muse inspired me."

A wan smile, and then Callie said, "Maybe your muse is always inspiring you. It's just that sometimes you can hear her better than others."

"I could use her right now, for sure! I have a little less than two hours to get this done. I have everything I need to finish it, but somehow I'm just not feeling it, and this material I'm putting together won't inspire anyone. As you reminded me earlier, even hard-nosed executives decide first based on emotion, justifying the decision based on logic. I have all the logic here, but the emotion isn't there yet."

"Maybe because *you're* not feeling it," she said. "If you don't feel it, it's hard to make someone else feel it."

"I think you're right, but I'm not sure how to gin up the feeling when it isn't there."

Callie looked off in the distance for so long that Dan almost asked if she was OK, when she turned to look directly into his eyes, narrowed her own, and said, "Can I ask you a personal question?"

"Depends on how personal. For instance, I don't mind telling you I like cheese better than pie."

"It's not personal like a secret or anything. Just a heart question."

Dan stopped kidding and returned her gaze. She seemed serious. "I can't guarantee I'll answer, but go ahead."

"It doesn't sound like your heart is in this. Do you *want* to do these speaking gigs?"

"Of course! I mean…. I've been doing this for so long. Plus, I get a lot of satisfaction out of seeing the light bulb go on for people."

"How long has it been since that was enough?"

Dan looked as if she had slapped him. *Enough? How could it not be enough? Is it?*

"Look, Dan. I'm not here to tell you what to do. I'm just a barista. Sometimes I like to give people ideas to test. But I can't help but wonder. I've seen people who keep doing something just because they've been doing it. The problem is not that the light has gone out of whatever they're doing, or at least it's not *only* that. It's that keeping on keeping on robs time they could put into doing what *does* light them up."

"I have to admit, I don't feel the satisfaction I once did. But is that reason enough to quit? My daddy raised me to stick with stuff, to not give up when things get tough. In fact, Angela Duckworth says grit is a key to success, the ability to persevere."

"That's true! I know Angela, and I would agree with her on that. But there's more to it than perseverance. She talks about passion as well. In fact, she says grit is perseverance in pursuit of a *worthwhile* goal. Sticking with something that doesn't matter to you, or doesn't matter as much as something else, isn't grit. It's just wasting your life."

She looked down at the table and said, "Can I borrow your sketchpad?" Dan passed the red book over to her. She opened it to a blank page and drew with a pen that seemed to materialize in her hand.

"While I'm more into the philosophies of the ancient Greeks, there's a surprising overlap with some of the thought systems that come from Asia. There's a concept that comes to us through Japan called *ikigai*. Have you heard of it?"

"I've seen references to it, but I'm not sure I get it."

She drew four overlapping circles, writing on the circles and the overlaps, explaining as she went.

```
                    Love
            Passion      Mission
      Good                      World
       at        Ikigai         needs
           Profession    Vocation
                   Others
                   value
```

"The concept actually comes from the Japanese island of Okinawa, which boasts some of the longest-lived people in the world. It's not the only factor in their long lives, but research suggests that having a sense of purpose in life, a sense of accomplishment in something that matters to you, is one factor in what Dan Buettner called 'blue zones.' The word translates to 'a reason for living.'"

"Now that you mention it, I've read Buettner's work. I remember that the people he studied came from all over the world, but they had several factors in common."

"Exactly. You can't attribute longevity and quality of life to just one factor, but this factor is one many people overlook. You can divide ikigai up into four areas of life. First, there's identifying what we love. Then there's what the world needs. Then what people will pay you for. Finally, there's what we are good at.

"There are overlaps between any two of these. Like here."

She pointed to the area where "what the world needs" and "what people will pay you for" overlapped and wrote "vocation."

"This is where almost any business book will tell you to start. Find a need and fill it. There are things the world needs, but that people aren't willing to pay for. You need both. That's enough to make a living. But ikigai suggests it's not enough to make a life."

Dan looked over the rest of the drawing and pointed to another overlap.

"What about this one between 'what we love' and 'what we're good at'?"

Callie wrote "passion" in that area and smiled. "Do you see what happens there when you leave out the other two circles?"

"Sure! Just because you love it and you're good at it doesn't mean the world needs it, and it certainly doesn't mean anyone will pay you for it!"

"Exactly. We could look at how any of these overlap, and we would need a three-dimensional model to illustrate overlaps between circles on opposite sides I can't get into a two dimensional drawing. Just because you don't see an area of overlap between 'what we love' and 'what you can get paid for' doesn't mean there isn't an overlap.

"But don't get tied up in the potential overlaps. The key is right here in the middle, where all four areas come together. That's your ikigai, your reason for living, for that sense of accomplishment. There is something for you, Dan. Something that you love, that the world needs, that you can get paid for, and that you are or can be good at. That's your ikigai."

She turned once again to Dan and looked deep into his eyes, as if she could see his soul.

"So let me ask you something. You said you don't know how to gin up the feeling when it isn't there. When you re-read something you wrote that *fits*, the way a properly sized hat *fits*, do you have to 'gin up' a feeling, or do you just feel it?"

"Well, of course, I don't have to work at it. The feeling is how I know it fits."

Callie arched her eyebrows, put her pen away somewhere, and headed toward the kitchen. Over her shoulder she said, "So expand that. If you're not 'feeling it' when you look at that marketing stuff, it may be because you're not looking at the right thing."

She disappeared through the door, but her aura remained. *Maybe I'm looking at the wrong thing,* he thought. *Of course.*

He knew he had decided. Now he just needed to justify it.

And I know just how to do it.

***

Callie had him questioning what he wanted for his business—heck, for his life! For sure, he wasn't feeling it, and Callie's diagram helped him see why. He had been working in an area that the world needed, that he was good at, and that at least some people would pay him for.

But did he love speaking? He wasn't sure. He thought maybe he just didn't want to be a quitter, especially after having put so many years into building his speaking business.

He *was* sure, though, that writing fit the love, need, and good at areas of the ikigai, and in the past had fit the get-paid-for category. Writing filled all categories.

But maybe I'm too old to start back on the writing track, he thought.

As he sipped his cooling (but still delicious) London Fog, insight hit him like pond ice cracking.

Dan knew deep down that income wasn't a real problem. He worried that retirement would leave him and his family short of funds, but that worry lingered as a legacy from his parents, survivors of The Great Depression and World War 2. That's why it surprised him when he and Grace sat down with a retirement counselor and realized they would actually be in good financial shape.

Grace didn't want him to stop working because she didn't want the blame if he was bored—or maybe because she feared having him underfoot all the time. (Dan grinned when he thought about that.) But he had the leeway to choose *how* he would work. After all, most of the Blue Zone elders kept working, though not out of economic necessity. They simply loved what they did.

That meant that getting old (or at least older) wasn't a bug. It was a feature. He had the freedom to take a chance, freedom he had not had since his youth.

So why not do what he loved? Dan owned a book entitled *Do What You Love and the Money Will Follow*. The title implied a false promise, made explicit in the ikigai diagram. Doing what you love doesn't guarantee financial success. Maybe, though, doing what you love fits what the old philosophers would call "necessary, but not sufficient." His passion guaranteed nothing regarding money, but it formed a solid foundation.

Dan made a couple of preliminary phone calls and then dialed Elizabeth Martinez, confirmed in his earlier insight. He didn't want to leave her in the lurch, but he told her he had realized he was not a good fit for her event, and he gave her the contact info for another speaker.

"She'll be perfect for you," he said. "Plus, I know she can travel without a problem. In fact, she loves hopping on a plane, even seems to relish getting through the TSA lines."

"Wow, Dan! I appreciate your honesty and your referral," Elizabeth said. "It shows you want to take care of us. I'll call as soon as we get off the phone."

"Great!" Dan said. "I checked with her before calling you, and she'll be expecting your call."

"We won't forget you, Dan. Again, thanks!"

***

Tuesday, May 30

Dan hadn't been to the library in three weeks. Along with The BB, the library served as a "third place" refuge, a place of quiet and focus with few interruptions, a place he could hear himself think.

Today, he wanted to do a little personal research, so he rewarded himself for making a decision.

He had a notion that made little sense, yet somehow did, and he couldn't shake it. To clear his head, Dan needed to dig into the name he had seen on Callie's license. "Calliope Anagnostopoulos." It was a mouthful and not typical of the Tennessee folks he knew. But it sounded Greek, and Dan knew nearby Knoxville had a sizeable population of folks with Greek ancestry.

He picked an unoccupied table and set up his laptop and sketchpad. He didn't know what he sought, but he preferred the old-fashioned feel of physical books when he started research on a project. However, he didn't mind speeding things up with a few basic searches first.

A simple Google search revealed Anagnostopoulos to be a family name for a few famous people. In fact, it was the original family name for Spiro Agnew, the disgraced Vice President of the United States under Richard Nixon. *Not very auspicious,* Dan thought, but a little deeper probing showed the name meant "reader" or "scholar," which certainly fit the Callie he knew. But "Calliope" nudged at him further. He thought he remembered the name from his junior high reading interests when he had spent hours poring through books about Greek and Roman culture and mythology.

Dan noticed Sharon, the longtime reference librarian, at her desk. Skilled as he was at using Google and lesser known search tools, he had always found Sharon and her co-workers extremely valuable in doing background research on any topic he could throw at them. Whether for a lecture for one of his classes, a pitch to a client, or a workshop he developed, Sharon always had insight into sources that he would otherwise have missed.

"What can I help you find today, Dan?" she asked when he approached the desk.

"I'm onto something a little different today, Sharon. What would you suggest as a good starting place for getting to know a little about Greek mythology?"

"Wow, that is different from your usual! Are you teaching a new college course next term? I can't imagine a corporate audience would find that scintillating."

"Nothing that complex. I'm working on what you might call a personal project. I just need a little background."

Sharon led him to a section of the reference titles only for use in the library, no checkouts allowed. "I think you'll find several helpful titles here. Let me know if you need any help with other resources. We have some online courses available for no charge through the library portal."

"Thanks a bunch! I think I can find what I need right here."

Dan began perusing the titles in the mythology reference section. He recognized a classic reference book, *Bulfinch's Mythology*. He followed the index entry to "Calliope," where he read: "The Muses were the daughters of Jupiter and Mnemosyne.... Calliope was the muse of epic poetry...."

He felt a slight rise of hair on the back of his neck. *Just a name that goes along with the family name quite well,* he thought.

Next to *Bulfinch* sat a promising-looking title: *Who's Who in Greek and Roman Mythology*. It had several hundreds if not thousands of entries in the index.

These Greek gods and demigods really got around, he thought.

Calliope received more space here, including a family tree, both ancestry and descendants. Her entry said, "Calliope was the Muse of epic poetry, telling of the heroes and their deeds; and she could also play any musical instrument."

Callie's parents named her aptly, he thought. *She's certainly been my muse lately.*

Dan turned back to *Bulfinch* again and flipped to the M's, looking up Muses. When a folded piece of paper fell out, it almost didn't surprise him.

"Dan," it said on the outside in the familiar handwriting, but he saw other print there as well. When he unfolded it, he found an old magazine ad for Welch's Seltzer on the back of another ad for Lucky Strike cigarettes ("It's Toasted!") from *Collier's Weekly*, dated in January 1920. Someone had torn it out with care to use for a brief note. They used the white space of the ads, but occasionally wrote over a face or a seltzer bottle.

You've put two and two together, Dan. That's excellent. It means more to you than if someone just told you "four." It's perfectly fine to get help from many sources. After all, none of us gets through life alone. But there's something satisfying about coming up with your own answer. Three-year-olds soak up information the way a black hole sucks in light, but they delight in figuring things out for themselves. Did you know Welch's Grape Juice solved a problem? Thomas Welch was a follower of a Methodist group that led the temperance movement and advocated the use of unfermented grape juice for church communion. But it was hard to get grape juice to *not* ferment. Welch came up with a commercially viable way of pasteurizing grape juice. He found the answer he needed, when he needed it.Nobody else can give you the answer to your reason for living, Dan. But if you keep digging, you will find your answer. It will feel like it was there all along, just waiting for you to uncover it, and in a way, that is true. An old Greek word now lives in modern English that represents this feeling: "Eureka!" It literally means, "I have found it!" No one can find it for you, although others can help you look. But you have to find it yourself.I don't think the owner of this magazine will mind me tearing out an ad page to leave you this note. I think about the time you find this note, you will also have found another important insight that has led you to a decision. Trust your knowing.

Dan carefully folded the magazine page back together put it into his tablet case. He pulled out his sketchbook and turned to his page of Callie notes. He wrote:

The fifth guideline: Look for the aha. Three-year-olds love learning, and they love it when they figure something out, like flipping on a light switch. When your "light bulb" goes on, it lights up your heart.

I'm not sure my light bulb has gone on, Dan thought. *But I'm almost certain I can feel the switch.*

Chapter Seven

The Beginning of the Ending

Monday, June 5

"So, let me get this straight," Ana said. "You think you have been unknowingly talking to a demigod who works as a barista in a coffee shop. She has convinced you to give up 30 years of developing a speaking practice just at the point where you could really make big bucks. You're going to go back to writing, something you really haven't been able to do for a decade because you've been too depressed. Is this a good summary?"

"Pretty close," Dan said. "I'm not sure a Muse is a demigod. And she didn't convince me, she just asked questions and made observations. And I doubt I'm about to make big bucks because, if you haven't noticed, nurses are getting harder and harder to find. I figure that even though I'm ready to retire from the college, I'm going to spend more time in Hope's room than on stage. Oh, and here's the big thing. I don't think I stopped writing because I was depressed. I think I was depressed because I stopped writing. But otherwise, yeah, spot on."

Ana sighed. They sat across from each other at The Blissful Bean, the first time they met in the same space in over three months. Telephone calls and Zoom meetings work fine, but some conversations need to happen in person over steaming cups of coffee.

Ana sat still for a time, looking into her cup to focus her thoughts. She took a slow sip, then said, "I hate to ask, but... have you told Grace about any of this?"

"Sure! I tell her everything! Well, I haven't told her about the Greek Muse thing yet. I'm still trying to wrap my head around that part. But I told her about the conversations, and how they helped me figure out what truly matters to me, not just what I think should matter."

"What does she think?"

"She's waiting to see what I'm going to do with it all. Let's face it, I've had lots of different 'enthusiasms' over the years. I can't blame her for taking a 'wait and see' approach. But this isn't a new enthusiasm. It's a rekindling of what has been there all along. I don't think I'm giving up anything; I think I'm just breathing again.

"Plus, this doesn't mean I'll quit speaking. You and I both know lots of speakers who write a book to support their speaking. I'm just going to use speaking to support the books I write. That's where I'm going next. Out of the hundreds of thousands of words

I've written, I've hardly ever drilled through the deep work of an entire book. I realize the whole industry has shifted since my last one, so this is like starting over again. But a lot of it feels like getting back on the bicycle after a long time away."

"So, what are you going to write a book about? Something to do with speaking?"

Dan looked at the red sketchbook on the table at his elbow. He flipped to the pages where he had been posting the insights that came out of his conversations with Callie and the mind maps around them. He smiled, then looked up at Ana.

"I think I have an idea for one."

He scratched through THE WAY OF THREE-YEAR-OLD WISDOM and wrote THE WAY OF THE THREE-YEAR-OLD WHY.

***

Tuesday, June 13

Dan carefully loaded the framed prints into the back of the van, propped up against Grace's wheelchair. He separated each from its neighbor with bubble wrap, leaving no chance of a shift in the load puncturing anything. Cardboard and glass protected the heavyweight paper within each, but framing them had cost a lot. Dan took no chances on damaging any of the beautiful renderings.

Most of the prints began life as photos Grace had taken in Cades Cove in the Great Smoky Mountains, and they would have been beautiful in raw form. *Grace has an eye for this sort of thing*, Dan thought. They resembled nothing like the touristy shots most people took on their cell phones, though Grace's phone photos typically rivaled those taken by a pro with a Hasselblad.

The prints included perfectly framed shots of the grist mill and the John Oliver cabin, as well as stunning photos of a bear and her cubs, with all three subjects looking right at the camera. Dan remembered she had taken the shot from a prudent distance with a telephoto lens, and had somehow captured the perfect moment.

Another featured deer wandering through one of the many graveyards in the Cove, with one deer appearing to reverently read the weather-worn engravings of a child's gravestone topped by a small lamb.

A close-up of a single drop of rain dangled from the tip of a tree leaf, almost alive as it prepared to leap to follow its fellows.

Those would have been impressive enough, but Grace had used her new graphics tablet to enhance the original images, bringing some colors out brightly and muting others, emphasizing just the right line here and deepening a shadow there.

"I'm really nervous!" Grace said when Dan got in and started the vehicle. "I've never displayed any of my art *anywhere* except home. I still can't believe the Blissful Bean manager wanted to hang these!"

"He would be crazy not to. You know how people like looking at the rotating exhibits here. Your prints will help draw people in, so people can enjoy a visual treat while enjoying a great cup of coffee. What a brilliant combination!"

"But it's always been someone else's pictures up there! Plus, the BB has always been more your place than mine. I certainly enjoy their coffee, but you have much more of a connection than I do."

"That doesn't matter. All I had to do was show Sean your prints on my phone, and he was all in."

"Well, I'm glad. I have to admit, though, I'm not just nervous about the hanging. I'm curious about this person you're going to introduce me to."

"You're going to love her. Remember, she's the one who suggested I talk to Sean about your art—I guess I must have mentioned it to her. And you can also thank her for getting me to figure out where I really need to spend my time. She has a lot to do with getting me started writing again—and for getting me to spend more time with you!"

"I'm withholding judgment on that." She smiled and arched her eyebrows. "Who knows? I may tire of having you around."

"You'll just have to take that chance. I'm enjoying all this time, and I'm glad you're going with me to the coffee shop. They'll know you as well as they know me."

They spent the next three hours carefully hanging framed prints on the walls of The Blissful Bean Coffee Haven, placing descriptive cards beside them in just the right place, straightening them to Grace's discerning eye. Dan kept watching for Callie, but he saw no sign of her.

Just as they finished, Sean came down the stairs and greeted them.

"Grace, these are really lovely! People are already walking around checking them out, and I saw several taking phone shots of your contact cards. I'm just amazed at the colors and the composition of your work!"

Grace blushed a little, but she smiled shyly. "Thanks! I'm just glad Dan talked with you about it."

"I'm not sure I would have thought of it, except Callie suggested I talk with you," Dan said. "Where is she today, by the way?"

"Who?"

"Callie. You know, she's a fairly new barista. I think she started about a month ago."

Sean looked confused. "I don't recognize that name, and we haven't hired anybody recently. What's she look like? Maybe she used a different name on her paperwork."

"I think you would recognize her. Sort of short, a little over five feet, I'd say. Dark red hair, shoulder length. She has a Greek script tattoo on her right wrist."

Sean shook his head. "Doesn't ring a bell. Hey, Tanner!" The young man behind the coffee counter looked up. "Do we have anyone named Callie working barista duty?"

Tanner looked thoughtful, shook his head. "No, I don't think so. Maybe she used to work here?"

"No," said Dan, "I only saw her for the first time maybe a month ago. In fact, I saw her in here two days ago."

"Sorry, man. I have no clue who you could be thinking of. Could it be Chelsea? She came here about six months ago, but you may not have noticed her." He turned toward the kitchen. "Hey, Chels! Got a minute?"

A young woman Dan recognized came out of the kitchen, drying her hands on a tea towel, wiping blond hair from her eyes and tucking it under a red bandana. Taller, blonder, fuller figure—not Callie.

"Hi, Chelsea," he said, "and thanks for playing the game, but you're not who I'm thinking of. Sorry. Any chance you've worked back there with someone named Callie?"

"Not been too many people working back here with me," she said, "and never anyone by that name since I've been here."

"Chelsea was our last hire," Sean said. "We're fortunate not to have had a lot of turnover in the last year or so. So I don't know who you might be thinking of. Whoever it was, I'm just glad you showed me Grace's pictures. Let Tanner know when you're done, and we'll treat you both to coffee."

Silence hung over them for minutes after Sean left, neither sure of what to say. Finally, Dan said, "I really don't know what to make of that. I mean, Callie suggested I get you the electronic sketch pad. She's the one who told me to talk to Sean. How could he not know who she is?"

Grace slowly shook her head. "Maybe she didn't actually work here? Maybe she was just another coffee lover who came here all the time?"

"But she went into the kitchen! She bussed tables! She even pulled coffee for me a couple of times. She *had* to have been working here."

"I don't know what to tell you, hon. I was really looking forward to meeting her, especially after all you've told me. I wanted to thank her for inspiring you—and for inspiring you to inspire me. But...."

Another patron came over to look at the print hanging on the wall behind them, a large print made from a photo Grace had taken in Cades Cove in the Smoky Mountains years ago. It featured a large maple tree in the center, isolated in a field close to the Cable Mill. Family tradition dictated she take a photo in the same location every time they made the trip through the Cove. This one, taken in the fall, showed the tree like an explosion of orange and yellow highlighted by a beam of sunlight. Grace had manipulated light and shadow to emphasize the tree while keeping the stunning mountain backdrop, and added acrylic paint embedded with carefully chosen bits of glass and aquarium gravel to bring the leaves to life. As a viewer moved around it, the "leaves" almost seem to shimmer in a mountain breeze.

"Isn't that gorgeous?" the woman said. "I've visited that place a dozen times, but I've never really seen it like this. The artist really has an eye!"

Dan smiled. "The artist is right here! Grace took the original photo and then applied her talents to enhance it."

"Really? How nice to meet you! Do you mind sharing how you achieved that wonderful sky?"

Grace and the woman happily began speaking the same language of graphics, color, and light as Dan backed away to read for a while. He kept looking around, though, hoping to glimpse the familiar Callie, hoping it was all just a misunderstanding.

As patrons realized Grace had made the stunning images on the wall, many stopped to talk with her about the prints and her process. They stayed until closing time with Grace graciously basking in the appreciation and Dan quietly taking it all in. He enjoyed seeing Grace in her element, but he also kept glancing toward the coffee bar and the kitchen doorway. In the occasional quiet lull, they studiously avoided talking about Callie, and by closing time, she still had not appeared, having vanished like the mist of the Great Smoky Mountains.

***

Wednesday, June 14

Dan just couldn't shake the Callie mystery. Grace had been understanding and supportive. *But a little condescending*, he thought, *as if I had imagined it all and couldn't separate reality from my own authorly thoughts.*

Could she be right? Maybe I did.

When he was younger, Dan would have gone for a walk in the woods to clear his head. The closest thing for him these days (*Grace isn't the only one with arthritis*) was a trip to the library.

And Dan had a lot to think about.

Grace had been more than supportive of his decision to relinquish the workshop opportunity with Elizabeth Martinez to another speaker. Dan decided that in the glow of what he considered an "aha" moment, the clarity that he needed to focus on his writing instead of putting so much time into trying to build a speaking business.

But that came before what he thought of as "the Callie mystery." It seemed no one had ever seen or even heard of Calliope Anagnostopoulos, a name that would stand out. The clarity of decision he had felt after working through the five guidelines of *The Way of the Three-Year-Old Why* had evaporated like so much incense smoke when he began to doubt whether any of it had happened—doubted his own sanity, if he was honest.

"Maybe I'm suffering from the effects of a lifetime of creative constipation," he told Ana. "Maybe I should have been writing all these years to give myself an outlet, and when I didn't, maybe my imagination got out of hand. Do you think I'm crazy?"

"Of course I do," she said. "I've known you too long to think anything else. But I don't think you're certifiable. I don't know what's going on with you, Dan, but you are one of the most level-headed people I know. I think you'll figure it out. You just have to give yourself space."

"Do you think it really happened?"

"I think *you* think it really happened. I think it opened up something in you that needed to open up. Honestly, I don't care about anything else. As someone once said, everyone needs to believe in something. I believe I'll have another beer, or in my case, another coffee."

As much as Dan needed another coffee, he felt reluctant to go back to The Bean. They still had the best coffee in town, but he thought they looked at him a little funny now when he came in. Maybe that, too, was his imagination, but it still didn't seem like the place for him at the moment.

That left the library.

Dan had to admit he loved the library just for being a library, amazingly well stocked and well run for a small town, with an enormous variety of fiction, nonfiction, and reference material. As much as he loved the access to information it provided, he appreciated the quiet spaces and comfortable environment where he could get away from everything to sit alone with his thoughts. He found both The Blissful Bean and the library great for working and creating, but nothing beat the library for slowing the pace of the world and allowing time and space to think.

As soon as he entered, Dan headed for a familiar section. He wanted to indulge his curiosity a bit, to head in a different direction than his usual, to give his mind a break. His professional interests often led him into the section on public speaking. It had been a long time since he had checked the adjacent section on writing for new books. He wanted to see what might catch his interest.

He came across a copy of a book that had long ago shaped his work, *On Writing,* by Stephen King. Even though he owned more than one copy, he hadn't read it in years, so he pulled it off the shelf to thumb through.

He settled into a comfortable chair that encouraged hours of reading and opened randomly to a page in the second half of the book, skimming familiar material. King expounded about plotting vs. discovery writing, the basic tools of vocabulary and grammar (while not getting overly concerned about either), and other writerly advice. Dan enjoyed it the way you enjoy a favorite song. Then he turned back to the beginning, slowing down to read again about King's early days working in a laundry to support himself and his family while he wrote stories published in magazines like *Dude, Cavalier, Adam,* and *Swank.*

Just as he reached the page where King described his beginning effort to write *Carrie*, something fell out of the book onto the floor.

Dan picked it up and froze. He held an envelope addressed to him, in the same handwriting that had been on the postcards, the magazine ads, and the napkin. No return address, no stamp, no postmark, but yellowed and sealed. The outside only bore a calligraphically printed name: his own. The envelope's imprint marked the pages that sandwiched it like a reverse shadow, appearing to have been there since the book's publication in 2000, though the envelope itself looked much older.

Dan knew the library collected things found in library books over the years, and that readers and would-be writers had to have checked out this well-thumbed book dozens of times over its life, and yet somehow the envelope seemed to have continued to live inside *its* pages from a time before he had even lived in the town.

With unsteady hands, Dan used his pocketknife to carefully slit open the envelope. He unfolded the paper inside as if it might break—the creases looked as if it would fall apart any second. Yellowed almost to the point of brownness, the paper seemed older even than the envelope. He unfolded it and found a watermark that said "J Whatman." A quick Internet search on his phone identified it as that of James Whatman, esteemed paper maker who invented "wove paper" and who died in 1759.

The writing had faded but clearly didn't come from a ballpoint. Elegant looping letters formed from lines all at once flowing but varying in thickness and depth, occasionally bleeding into the rough texture of the old paper, like letters he had seen in a museum.

He feared it might fall apart in his hands, but he pulled out his glasses and read the first line: "Dear Dan."

He carried the paper almost reverently to a nearby table and carefully laid it out to read.

> Dear Dan,
>
> Yes, it all happened. Don't try too hard to figure out the how. As you might know by now, a far more important question than "how" is "why."
>
> Depending on how you look at it, we last conversed a couple of weeks ago, or a couple of centuries from when I'm writing this. I don't experience time the way you do. I don't quite understand it myself. But

THE WAY OF THE THREE-YEAR-OLD WHY

I know my why, and I hope you know yours a little better now.

It has been my honor to serve as your Muse. Despite how some may look at the process of creation, it's not true that your ideas and creativity come to you through me or my sisters. You are far more than a simple pipeline, a taker of dictation. Our jobs resemble more that of a midwife, helping you bring forth what you are meant to bring forth.

In fact, you and I have talked one way or another your whole life. My sisters and I talk with humans all the time. It's just that some hear us better than others, and some talk back with us better than others. Thank you for that, by the way. I can't remember when I've had a more satisfying time (and, yes, that's a pun) talking with a musee.

But we won't talk quite that way any more—because we don't need to. I will still be with you, not doing your work for you, but helping you bring it forth. You have contributions to make to the world. Your contributions come through writing. Some people, like Grace, make the world a better place through their vision and graphics (not yet a common word as I write this). Some people do it through their elegant solutions in plumbing. (Do you realize how much plumbers have done to make life easier, longer, and healthier?)

And I have to tell you this: you have known since your childhood this was your work, and you let your fear impede pursuing it. Just as you should not waste time trying to determine how recent experience "really" happened, you should not waste time beating yourself up for the years you did something other than write. Perhaps it represents a lost opportunity that you cannot get back. But in a much more important way, it was incubation.

Does a bird regret the time spent inside its egg? When a robin lays her eggs, she tends to them for a time. She presses against them to warm them, or spreads her wings to shade them and cool them to just the right temperature. She moves them and rotates them to make the temperature even and to keep the embryos from sticking to their shells. They do not go straight from delivery to hatching. They need incubation.

During those two weeks, much happens that no one can see. When they hatch, they do not waste energy regretting those 14 days. They get on with the business of eating, growing feathers, and fledging.

Then one day they fly.

Of course, this is an imperfect metaphor, because you *have* been writing all along, except for that long stretch when you weren't. You just were not writing what you wanted, what you were meant to. You have been like a chicken in a barnyard. Contrary to popular belief, chickens actually *can* fly. But they only fly for short distances, and then only far enough to get some food.

There is nothing wrong with that. Chickens contribute to the world too! Robins look down on chickens only in a physical, literal sense.

But a robin that spends its life believing itself a chicken will not thereby become a happy chicken.

You have robin work to do. You will make the world a better place through your work. You've made a solid start on your book. You may think of it as our book, but it's not. You're taking timeless, universal ideas and putting them in a form only you can shape. Though I will accompany you in a much quieter way from here on, I want to share one last bit of advice with you: get out of your own way. Humility does not mean denying your abilities. It means using your gift to benefit your world.

You have heard the message I wanted to help you shape, a message from within yourself, and you have put that message in a form the world needs to hear. Many people my sisters and I know need to learn how to find their own particular "why" the way a three-year-old would. Take that message to them.

By the way, before you leave this repository of books, go over to the shelves numbered 752 and find a book by another musee of mine, Betty Edwards, about color. Thumb through that and you'll find another envelope addressed to Grace. Do me a favor and take that to her, will you? There is a reason that you need to be the one to deliver it to her, a reason that will bind the two of you even closer together. But note: that envelope is for her, not for you. Let her read it in private and share it with you in her own time.

I'll see you on the page.

This time, the letter ended with a signature of sorts.
"Love always, Callie, a.k.a. Calliope Anagnostopoulos, Carmenta, Bragi, Saraswati, Brigid, Ptah, Benzaiten, Kokopelli,

Hinewai, Sága, and some other names I have forgotten—names that don't matter, as long as you remember your own."

Dan refolded the quarto paper back just as it was, slowly put it back into its envelope, and returned to his chair to sit for a couple of minutes looking at it, almost expecting it to evaporate or self-destruct like a *Mission Impossible* tape.

"Hey, Dan," said a contralto voice behind him.

With a start, Dan whipped around.

It was Sharon, his reference librarian friend.

"Don't look so disappointed, Dan," she said with a smile. "Were you expecting somebody else?"

Dan looked a little sheepish. "Sorry about that, Sharon. No, actually, I'm glad to see you. This is going to sound a little weird, but I'd like you to do me a favor. See this envelope? Can you tell me what it says on the front?"

"Oh, are you going to a wedding? You rarely get your name on an envelope like that in such beautiful script. Where's the outer envelope?"

"What outer envelope?"

"The one with the address on it. Last time I got one like that, my cousin paid big bucks to mail out all these fancy invitations. It was like one of those Russian nesting dolls, envelopes inside envelopes. Had an intricate wax seal on the outside, and calligraphy on each envelope. No computer printing for that one!"

"This is all I have. But, and don't think I'm crazy for asking, do you see my name on this envelope?"

Sharon looked puzzled. "Of course, silly. Who else's name would be on it? Better get a nice present for that one. By the way, how's the research going for that Greek thing you were looking at?"

"I think it has taken a rather... *interesting* turn. I'll tell you about it as soon as I figure out what it is."

Dan tucked the envelope in with all his previous notes and gathered his materials.

But first, he headed over to the 720s in the stacks. *I can't wait to see Grace's face when I hand her whatever I find in that book,* he thought.

Chapter Eight

The Five Guidelines

1. **Look for the curiosity.** Look at the world the way a three-year-old does, as if everything is new. Honor your wonder.

2. **Look for the "so that."** A three-year-old doesn't stop with the first answer. He still wants to know "why." What's the outcome?

3. **Look for the emotion.** A three-year-old mainly responds to emotion, as we all do. He just doesn't hide it. Without emotion, there is no motion.

4. **Look for the story.** Three-year-olds love stories, just as we all do. A story brings together emotion and reasoning to create meaning. Find the story, create the story, and you will find meaning.

5. **Look for the aha.** Three-year-olds love learning, and they

love it when they figure something out, like flipping on a light switch. When your "light bulb" goes on, it lights up your heart.

Author's Notes

Note before notes: as a thank you for purchasing this book, you can download a bonus chapter by going to https://BookHip.com/QQPRGRT.

Future editions of this book will call this part "Frequently Asked Questions" or FAQ. But since, as I write this, the book is just about to be published, there are no FAQs yet. This note, therefore, answers some questions I anticipate readers might have, and it's tucked in the back to avoid spoilers for those who don't want to know until they come across it.

For whatever it's worth, I confess to having a tendency to turn to the back of the book to see how it turns out before I read it. I take pleasure in seeing how an author gets to the resolution, so spoilers do not spoil a book for me—I just want to know whether characters I care about are going to survive or not so I can prepare.

Dear Reader, if you are of a different mind and have not read the story yet, turn away now. Spoilers lie ahead.

Some of this you can glean from the Acknowledgements page, but we'll make it explicit here. The Blissful Bean is modeled on but not identical to a real coffee shop in Maryville, Tennessee, called

Vienna Coffee. The physical description of the BB matches Vienna closely. The baristas other than Callie represent the many who work at Vienna, with one of those supporting characters having the same name as an actual barista—an Easter egg for locals to enjoy. Another Easter egg concerns one of the regular patrons. As far as we know, however, Vienna doesn't employ a barista only Dan can see.

Speaking of Dan, yes, I worked a lot of my experience into Dan's. But he is not simply me. He is a little younger than me, and definitely in better physical shape, though we're both tired. I modeled Grace on my wife, whose challenges include debilitating arthritis. Both my wife and I have several other physical challenges too complex to include in a relatively short book, so Dan's and Grace's challenges are simpler.

My wife is genuinely wildly creative, and we both have done professional-level photography in years past. But my wife's creativity gets expressed regularly through crochet instead of painting. Though she painted many years ago, she has not been drawn to painting in recent years (see what I did there?). But the photographs described in the story are based on actual shots she took in Cades Cove, and the wood-carving story is almost 100 percent real as well.

The conversation in the hospital where we discussed the possibility of donating our daughter's organs happened in real life. Thankfully, just as with Hope, our daughter lived. The description of her disability also closely resembles Hannah's actual situation.

I was making substantial progress as a keynote speaker when Hannah came along, and so I relate to Dan in that way. Unlike Dan, the pandemic actually helped me increase business. When the rest of the world went on Zoom, suddenly I could schedule speeches on the same basis as other professional speakers. I delivered several keynotes and programs from Hannah's room. Dependable nursing enabled me to give several in-person speeches later, after the pandemic waned.

Like Dan, I switched back to emphasizing writing. Unlike Dan, it didn't happen because of endangered gigs. My real-life Muse didn't come in the form of anyone resembling Callie. The closest such person was Jeff West, who wrote the foreword for this book. Once I started writing again, I actually told him I had thought I wasn't writing because I was depressed, whereas I figured out I was actually depressed because I wasn't writing.

We mention a couple of times that Dan teaches college, but it doesn't seem a big part of his life. In real life, I have worked with college students as well as leaders and professionals for over 40 years, and it has formed a large and satisfying foundation for a career. I have to admit that if things had gone according to plan, I probably would have left academia 15 to 20 years ago. But I have always enjoyed teaching, and the college has always supported me in balancing taking care of Hannah and taking care of my students.

In the early draft of this book, I realized Callie and her sisters have more to say, and so *The Way of the Three-Year-Old Why* became the first book of **The Sparklight Chronicles**.

I hope you enjoyed both the book and these extra insights. Keep an eye out for the next book in the series, working titled Real Speak. You'll find the first chapter in a few pages. Stay in touch!

Discussion Guide

Many readers may want to explore *The Way of the Three-Year-Old Why* together in their book clubs, business study groups, houses of worship and community groups, or among friends and family. The questions below may help in guide your discussions.

1. You may or may not relate to Dan's dilemma of needing to balance caretaking with making a living. If so, what have you learned about such balancing? If not, what is another situation in which you have felt stuck?

2. Has there been a time in your life when it helped to have someone to listen to you and reflect with you? If so, what was it? If not, was there a time when you wish you had had such a person?

3. What are some complications in the relationship between Dan and Grace?

4. Callie tells Dan, "You can't pour from an empty pitcher." Is that something you need to hear? Where might the

insight be helpful to you?

5. When was the last time you indulged your curiosity?

6. What limitations or barriers do you have in reaching a goal that matters to you? What is something that could help you manage or overcome those limitations or barriers?

7. What once made your heart sing? Does it still?

8. If you got sidetracked, how did that happen? Are you still trying to find the track? What do you know about it at this point?

9. What is a "so that" that actually matters to you?

10. When you experience emotion, how do you deal with it? Do you express it somehow? Do you push it away? Do you put it in charge?

11. Think about a time emotion impeded something you wanted to do. Now think about a time emotion gave you the energy to do something difficult. What does this tell you about the role of emotion in your life?

12. Have you thought of satisfaction as an emotion? How might that understanding affect your life goals? Will achieving those goals lead to satisfaction?

13. Conflict and challenge lie at the heart of every good story,

but in "real life" many of us avoid conflict and challenge. How has your approach to conflict affected your life?

14. Stories go beyond "this happened, then that happened." They involve a character facing a challenge who grows as a result. Another fictional character, the 11th Doctor in the Doctor Who series, once said, "We are all stories in the end, just make it a good one, eh?" What insight does that quote give you into your own life?

15. What is something you believe would help you achieve your goal that scares you? What is a baby step toward that scary action?

16. What story have you told to explain why you "can't" do something that matters to you? What different story could you tell (or that you have already told) to empower you to overcome the challenge? Sometimes a story involves a character discovering they didn't really want their original goal, but wanted something else more deeply. Do you have a story like that?

17. If you were already familiar with the concept of *ikigai*, where have you identified something missing in your life? If *ikigai* is a new idea for you, how do your various activities look when mapped onto the four circles?

18. Think about a decision you once fretted over. What enabled you to finally decide? How did you feel once you

decided?

19. What does the term "buyer's remorse" mean to you? Do you second guess your decisions?

20. Looking back over the book, what do you wish you knew more about? What unanswered questions do you have?

First chapter of Real Speak

The next book in the Sparklight Chronicles

One thing Harold knew for sure. Visualizing them naked didn't work. In fact, it had the opposite effect—trying to do so just made *him* feel naked.

Still, he knew he had done his homework, that he knew all the facts he needed to present, and that he had plenty of data on his slide deck to back himself up. He also knew that if he had any hope of moving up in the organization, he had to get past the memories and at least tolerate speaking to the other supervisors.

I've got this, he thought to himself. *They're always telling you to think positive. So I'm thinking positive. I've got this.*

He took a deep breath, picked up the clicker, and launched into it.

"How's everyone doing today?" he said.

Sam Jennings, sitting in the front row, sighed almost imperceptibly and sneaked a look at her watch. Some of the others stirred, and a couple mumbled things like, "Fine." "Good." "OK."

"Well, let's get right into it, then. I have a lot of information to share with you, and I know I'm standing between you and lunch. You'll notice from this chart that in the third quarter our project revenue was good, but it was down about 4 percent compared to the same period a year ago...."

***

This could have been an email, Sam thought. She had already seen Harold's written report. *Why do I have to waste time sitting through yet another boring meeting?*

Sam doodled on her legal pad, hoping it looked as if she were taking notes. Sitting on the front row had probably been a mistake, but he wanted to be visible to the C Suite folks. She had seen Elizabeth Martinez quietly slip into the back row, and she knew if she wanted to move up, she had to been seen as a leader.

Sam certainly wanted to move up. She knew the C's talked a lot about leadership, and she understood the term, at least in a dictionary sort of way. She just couldn't quite wrap her engineer's brain around such a fuzzy concept.

Materials specifications, she understood. Spreadsheets made sense. Math worked the same every time. But people? People made less sense than silly putty.

As Harold droned on about the division's earning, Sam's mind wandered back to a conversation with Martinez at the end of last year.

"No one can top you for tech knowledge, Sam, and you're the best when it comes to troubleshooting projects," she said. "I really want to bring you up into higher leadership, but there's a bit of a problem. We've had this conversation before, and since I come from an engineering background and I also relate to the challenges of being a woman in a highly male-dominated field, I think I can understand why those conversations haven't led to the hoped-for outcome."

Sam had listened intently, disappointed but determined to solve this problem the way she solved geometric dimensioning and tolerancing equations or figured out a new feature on the CAD software.

"Because of that, I know you probably don't want to hear this, just like I once didn't want to hear it," Martinez continued. "And just like I needed to hear it clearly, without ambiguity, I'm going to tell you plainly: you will advance no further, in this company or almost any other, unless you gain some measure of 'people skills.'"

"You mean like the marketing folks use? That's just so much sleazy, fuzzy fluff!"

"One of the first thing you have to learn about it is that sleazy doesn't cut it. And although you can't count it the way our accounting folks count dollars *or* our design folk measure failure rates, it is far from fluff. Solid, scientific studies support the impact of of effective communication strategies."

Sam scoffed. "Scientific studies? If you're talking about focus groups and so-called 'qualitative studies,' I would hardly call them scientific."

"Call it what you will. The results can be replicated. The fact that you're arguing with it shows the basic problem. Again, I'll state it plainly: getting over that kind of attitude was the linchpin that changed my career. Do you have any idea how rare it is for an engineer to become a VP of Sales for any major corporation? Fewer than 10 percent. Want to guess how many of those are female? We're out there, but we're almost unicorns. You don't have to pursue that C-Suite office. There are others. But until you understand sales and marketing, you have no hope of getting beyond your current level.

"And sales and marketing means you have to understand people. By the way, if you understood even the basics of dealing with people, you probably wouldn't disparage the marketing folks when you're talking to the marketing person most in a position to help you."

Sam looked shocked and began to stammer, "Oh! I'm sorry! I didn't mean to.... I mean, it didn't, um, I meant, ah.... Really, I'm sorry, I wasn't thinking."

"Yes, you were. You were thinking. You were thinking exactly the way you have always thought—like an engineer. That's not a bad thing at all. I don't want you to stop thinking like an engineer. It's not a matter of either-or. It's both-and.

"Here's the thing, Sam. As an engineer, you have an advantage for the C-Suite. You know how to analyze problems and determine criteria for the solution. You know how to gather and analyze data. You can take complex ideas and break them down into logical components. All of that is necessary for success in any 'Chief' position. It's just not sufficient, not without the people skills. Why do you think you have so much turnover in your section?"

"I think we keep hiring people who can't handle the feedback they need to hear."

"We're losing good people, Sam, and our competitors are hiring a lot of them after they leave us. They manage to thrive at other companies, a lot of them. Do you think those companies just don't give them the feedback they need?

"No, I'm sorry, Sam. You can't blame the people. We're hiring the best raw talent out there, and they need a leader. A leader. Not a manager. A leader. That's going to take people skills."

Martinez stood up, and so did Sam. "We've hired a consultant. You're not the only supervisor having this problem, so we want her to work with several of you. But, Sam, you have to take her seriously. And I mean, seriously. We don't just hire talented designers. We hire talented designers with potential. That's why you're here. You have the potential to truly lead.

"But potential doesn't always pan out. That's why we're bringing in a consultant name Ama Terasu. You may not have heard of her, but she's the one who guided me when I was in your shoes. I know you have a supervisor's meeting to attend, so I'll let you go. When she calls you this afternoon, do us both a favor: take her call, and make sure you pay attention to what she tells you. Deal?"

Sam swallowed hard, but she looked back at Martinez steadily and said, "Deal. Thank you for believing in me."

Martinez looked grim. "Justify it. I know you can. I'm waiting to see if you will."

"Anyone have any questions?" Harold said.

Sam snapped back to the present. She looked around quickly, saw Martinez in the back row looking straight at her. She studied her legal pad, now covered with geometric figures and quadratic equations, as if seeking a note. Harold looked around hopefully as silence held. People began to squirm and check cell phones. After a long silence, Harold said, "Well, I guess that means we covered everything. No questions? All right, good, well, um, everyone have a good rest of your day."

Sam's phone buzzed. She checked the text and saw that it was from A. Terasu. "Good time to chat?" the text said. *Guess I'd better get to the office. I really don't want anyone else hearing this conversation.*

***

The time flew by for Harold, and he barely had a memory of what he had said and done. But he knew he had covered all the material, and he had kept it under an hour. In fact, he had sped through the material in only 40 minutes, which he figured would be a relief to the other supervisors. After all, Harold knew how many meetings he himself had sat through hoping that they would soon be over.

As he carried his laptop down the hall toward his cubicle, Harold nearly crashed into Elizabeth Martinez coming out of the break room.

"Whoa!" he said as he tried not to knock her coffee cup from her hand. *It's probably not a good idea to cream your Vice President*, he though, but he said, "I'm really sorry! I should have been watching more closely. My apologies!"

She had looked startled, but Martinez recovered quickly. She always seemed to maintain her cool no matter what happened, a trait Harold sought to emulate with varying success.

"No harm, no foul," she said. "I'll bet you were thinking about the presentation you just gave."

"Were you there?"

"You bet. That project is an important one."

It was Harold's turn to look startled. He had not noticed Martinez, but it probably was a good thing he had not. His nervousness would have gone up like a fourth of July rocket. Still, it turned out to be an opportunity. He knew he had given a clear picture of just exactly what the project challenges were.

"Do you mind if I ask you what you thought? I'm open to feedback."

Martinez looked at him for a thoughtful moment, then said, "Are you sure?"

"I'm sorry?"

"Are you sure you're open to feedback? Let's be honest. Most people to really want feedback. They just want to be told what a good job they did."

Harold swallowed, but plowed ahead. "I would appreciate any genuine observations you can make. I think."

"Why?"

Stuttering just a little, Harold replied, "I really want to move up in the company. I need to have an accurate idea of how I'm doing if I am going to do that, and I can't think of a better person to give me that, if you're willing, than my VP. So give me the bad news. I can handle it."

She chuckled. "Don't assume it's bad news. But it probably deserves more than a hallway conversation. How about this? There's a Toastmasters club that I know about that meets on Wednesday mornings at the coffee house a couple of blocks over. Why don't you check them out tomorrow morning, and meet with them for two or three weeks. Maybe even join. Then you can tell me how you think you did. You can even watch the recording."

"Recording?"

"Sure. You didn't know we were recording the presentation? As I said, it's an important project."

The thought of listening to himself talk filled Harold with dread, but he didn't think that was a smart revelation to the boss. He just said, "That's great! It certainly gives me an opportunity for growth."

Or humiliation. Maybe it will just prove I'm not promotable.

"Perfect," she said. "See you in the morning, then. I'll email you the address."

She'll be there too? What have I gotten myself into?

***

Keep up with Harold's journey *and* Sam's journey. Get notified when *Real Speak* comes out. Connect with us at DonnKing.com/RealSpeak.

Acknowledgements

An artist of any kind is not simply a conduit, but on the other hand the creation depends on many people, not just one (in this case) writer. I owe a great deal of gratitude to the following people who helped to midwife the book you are currently holding.

Jessica Hannah, coffee marketing guru, for her insight into the operations of a coffee shop.

John Clark and all the folks at Vienna Coffee House for their wonderful roastery and café, the inspiration for the setting, the atmosphere, and the people.

Jeff West, co-author of *Said the Lady with the Blue Hair*, for his support and encouragement, and especially for his insightful feedback on the writing of a business fable.

Bob Burg, co-author of the series that began with *The Go-Giver*, for his long friendship and encouragement in writing and living the 5 Laws of Stratospheric Success. He is the master of the business parable/fable, and his feedback was invaluable.

Beta readers Amy Bivens, Rebecca Griffith, Jenn Haston, and Wil Davenport, all of whom took the time to give detailed feedback and help me find holes and missteps.

The Go-Giver Success Alliance, a wonderful community of people dedicated to living by those principles.

The good folks at UPS Store #3376 in Alcoa, TN, for their insight and advice on modern options for art prints. You pointed me in the right direction.

Don Brown, who appears in this book. You are gone but not forgotten. Dear Reader, every word herein about Don Brown is true.

Diane Benson, the real-world reference librarian at the Blount County Public Library who helped me find the background information for the historic information herein.

Alexandra Watkins, "Brand Name Badass" and author of Inc. Top 10 Marketing Book, *Hello, My Name is Awesome: How to Create Brand Names That Stick*, who helped me come up with the name for the series this book starts (the Sparklight Chronicles) as well as the name for my publishing imprint (Hidden Mentor Media).

Especially to my wife, Janet. You and our children have given me my core for the foundation of my ikigai. There is Amanda, the oldest, to whom I told some of my first stories. There is Zach, the protector of so many and so much. There is Cate, the middle child, who has come so far on a rough road. I must mention two of our children in particular, not because they are favorites (all my children are my favorite), but because of their special circumstances. There is Hannah, the inspiration for Hope, who cannot speak back to me, but to whom I will read this book. And there is Barry, the oldest son who left this world in January 2018. Son, you may not be here for me to hand you a copy, but you are scattered throughout this book. You made me proud, and I hope this story makes you proud of me.

About the Author

Donn is an associate professor of communication studies at Pellissippi State Community College in Knoxville, Tennessee, and a pastor in the United Methodist Church, as well as a speaker, writer, and communication coach.

Donn King

He works with professionals and leaders who want to speak confidently so they can increase their impact, gain influence, and build their careers.

He has spoken to audiences, churches, and radio audiences across the United States and written numerous newspaper, magazine, and blog articles. He authored *The Right-brained Guide to Parliamentary Procedure: A Path Through the Forest* and co-authored *Responsibly Spoken*, a textbook on public speaking. His latest book is *The Way of the Three-Year-Old Why*, the first book in the Sparklight Chronicles.

Donn is a proud member of The Go-Giver Community and The Go-Giver Success Alliance with Bob Burg and Kathy Tagenel. He has been a guest on podcasts and shows such as *Write Your Book in a Flash* hosted by Dan Janal, *Business Inspiration* hosted by Dana Morgan Barnes, The *Be Better Broadcast* hosted by Brandon Eastman, and *The Nashville Association of Sales Professionals* hosted by Terry Lancaster.

For over 40 years, Donn has taught college students and business leaders the skills of effective communication. In recent years, he has guided dozens of professional speakers, teachers, and presenters in the effective use of Zoom for engaging communication. He is the winner of the Excellence Award and the Innovation Award, both from the National Institute for Staff and Organizational Development.

He has earned a B.A. in communications from Freed-Hardeman University in Henderson, Tennessee, and an M.S. in communications from the University of Tennessee, Knoxville.

Donn is married to Janet. Together they have five children, four of whom survive, three of whom are grown and independent, and one of whom is... complicated. Donn and Janet live on the quiet side of the Great Smoky Mountains, where Donn teaches and writes, and Janet makes amazing creations from yarn, and where they enjoy the best coffee in Tennessee.

Special coffee offer

You can tell that coffee figures heavily into this book, and it does so throughout **The Sparklight Chronicles**. We have worked out a special deal with one of the real-life inspirations for coffee and coffee shops that appear throughout the series. At publication, the nature of that was still evolving, but if you love your coffee, you will want to go to

DonnKing.com/coffee

to see what goodies come along with your purchase of this and other books in **The Sparklight Chronicles** series. The offerings will almost certainly evolve over time. That means a) you will want to check back for new offerings, and b) you will want to grab what looks good to you now, since nothing guarantees the continuation of any particular offering on that page.

Made in the USA
Columbia, SC
28 January 2024